Guilty or not Guilty?

Murder in the Upper Hunter

1837 - 1849

Rob Tickle

ETT IMPRINT
Exile Bay

Rob Tickle

About the author:

Rob Tickle has a BA (UNE) in archaeology, palaeoanthropology and history along with an Associate Diploma in Local and Applied History (UNE) and a postgraduate certificate in Historical Archaeology (University of Leicester). He has had a lifelong passion for history, but over the past thirty years, his main interest has been local history in the Hunter Valley and family history. He is a member of the Port Macquarie Historical Society, Wauchope & District Historical Society, life member of Muswellbrook Shire Local & Family History Society Inc., and member of the International Golden Keys Society. For a number of years, he has worked as a consulting archaeologist and historian in New South Wales and Western Australia.

First published by ETT Imprint, Exile Bay in 2026

ETT IMPRINT
PO Box R1906
Royal Exchange NSW 1225
Australia

Typeset by Veritas Archaeology & History Service

ISBN 978-1-923527-27-0

Cover design by Tom Thompson

TABLE OF CONTENTS

PROLOGUE
Between 1837 and 1849 25 men died in the Upper Hunter, not from a visitation of God, but by the hand of man.

None made three score and ten years before death arrived, some of the deaths show the influence of the Devil.

How did these men die? The first met death from a drunken fight that he had started; the next is a mystery, but his body was found with the skull fractured. Rum had a bearing on the next, having a yard of your intestines hang out of a cut in the groin did not auger well for a long life. His death resulted in another being hung by the law. Murder was a capital crime [a capital crime was any that was punishable by death[1]]. A constable lost his life when shot in the line of duty, the suspect dodged the noose; he was never found.

A servant was shot while defending his master which resulted in two of the assailants being hung, but there was another death associated with this incident. While the bushrangers were on the run, the leader of the gang killed an associate.

A storekeeper died after being shot by bushrangers, one man was hung for murder and five more for aiding and abetting. The next death of a constable, resulted from a gunshot wound while doing his duty, in this case the perpetrator was hung. More mystery with the next death, officials had a body that died of a knife wound, but could not determine the identity of the victim. No one was ever charged with the crime.

Two Aboriginals were killed by brethren, but no one was brought to trial. In the next case a man was found with head wounds in a shallow grave, a suspect was charged with murder but eluded the hangman.

Another died as a result of a knife wound to the stomach inflicted during a quarrel, again the other man was charged with murder, but found guilty of the lesser crime – manslaughter. Next a body was found with the skull fractured by an axe or stone. A person was charged with the crime, found guilty and hung.

The last had his head caved in with a tomahawk, the person responsible turned himself in. He pleaded self-defence, but was charged with murder. He escaped the noose.

So, in a 12-year period 25 men died in the Upper Hunter, NSW from a violent action.

Settlement
The following is a brief overview of the development of the area so you can understand the locality of the deaths and how people endured the isolation and lack of facilities.

While Newcastle remained a penal settlement there was very little activity further out in the Hunter Valley. All that changed following the closure of Newcastle in 1823. Settlement of the valley was made available to person with capital. Henry Dangar, government surveyor was working in the Hunter Valley during 1822-23 while Alan Cunningham travelled from Bathurst to the Goulburn River, a tributary of the Hunter, in 1825 and published glowing reports on the potential of that valley.

Muswellbrook was surveyed in 1833 with land sales the following year, Scone surveyed 1837 and Murrurundi in 1840. By the early 1830s the best land along the Hunter had been taken up for grazing properties.

Travel was difficult in the area, while it was possible to use the Hunter, Williams and Paterson Rivers in the lower Hunter, river travel was not possible elsewhere. Transport was by foot, horse or dray over unmade roads or tracks.

Land was obtained by grant and the size of the grant was based on the capital the settler held. The number of convicts assigned also depended on the level of capital. Generally, the early settlers were men of substance and standing including retired naval and military officers. The 1828 Census indicated that 42% of the land was managed by Overseers for non-resident owners. In the same census, 69.3% of the population in the Hunter were convicts who formed a large proportion of the population. Under Governor Brisbane landholders were allowed one convict for each 100 acres granted, though often the Government could not supply this number[1].

Many of the owners were made magistrates and formed a bench with local courts. These courts developed on stations before government villages came into being. Two examples are Merton the station of William Ogilvie and

[1] The UK, in early 1800s has 220 crimes punishable by death. Many of these the offences were an attempt to protect the wealthy class. Between 1770 and 1830 an estimated 35,00 death sentences were handed down in England and Wales of which 7000 were carried out. This is the law that was brought to Australia with Governor Phillip and the First Fleet. During the 19th century, crimes that could carry a death sentence included burglary, sheep stealing, forgery, sexual assault, murder and manslaughter. Homosexual activity remained a capital offence until 1867. The last execution in Australia took place in 1967, when Ronald Ryan was hanged for killing a prison officer at Pentridge Prison.

Cassilis, station of Alexander Bushby. Both men erected buildings for courts, lock-up and accommodation for police at their own expense. These sites developed into private villages.

Life on a station

Life on the early stations was harsh, especially for a convict. Most were allocated the position of shepherd or watchman.

The owner on receiving his land grant would establish the head station of homestead, store, blacksmith shop and accommodation for staff based there. Around his run there would be small huts, outstations, where two shepherds and a watchman would live and look after the sheep. The shepherd would have 500 plus sheep to tend. They would be out at daylight and back at sunset. Sheep were put into yards and the watchman would take over. Diet was poor, rations were delivered to the hut once a week and a typical fare would be 10lbs meat (usually salted), 10lbs flour, 3oz tea and sugar. All depended on the master.

The standard of discipline varied from station to station. Large station could have a farm constable employed by the owner who would escort refractory convicts to the closest Bench for what would be considered minor misdemeanours but then loss of a sheep or insolence could result in 25 to 50 lashes. The total boredom drove some mad.

A sentence of transportation could be for 7 years, 14 years or life. With good behaviour a convict could be given a reduced sentence and be issued with a ticket of leave. This allowed him to work in a designated district on his own account. Eventually he may have earned a conditional pardon which would have made him a free man within the colony.

This was life for many and may have been the cause for some of the murders you will read about.

INTRODUCTION

Why write a book on murder? Murder was (and probably still is) a sensational crime that attracted widespread interest within the community, not only within the locality where the murder took place, but also in the much wider community of Australia. Often the newspapers of other states reported the details of the murder and the trial if one took place.

Executions were still held publicly, so murder stories were followed with special interest. The case might end in an execution and the public looked on the spectacle akin to going to the colosseum. Even women and children were allowed to view the spectacle of a hanging.

As a local and family historian, I am often trying to find information on people who have not made the mainstream records. In the early period of our European history in Australia, it can be very difficult to find information on people who came to an area and just went about their normal lives. Sometimes no marriages, baptisms or deaths occur during their period of residence within an area. If they were law abiding, God-fearing residents then their names may not appear in any records.

This is why murder trials are so valuable for local and family historians. Your person of interest may have been called to give evidence as a witness. This is the interesting part, on entering the witness stand they would have given their name plus an alias if they were using one, occupation and whom their employer was. This was information under oath and there were very stiff penalties for lying in the stand.

There are often interesting descriptions of buildings, towns and the general countryside. This can yield valuable information on social conditions giving us an insight into how people lived, ate and drank. Gin and rum were favoured alcohol. People often walked from town to town and camped in the bush. A coat would have far greater value than now and many travelled light with a change of one or two shirts. The clothes of the murdered person are often described in detail.

There is still the morbid fascination into murder today as there was 170 years ago. Why does a person go forth without the fear of God before their eyes and being influenced by the Devil, take another person's life? Revenge, greed, passion? After reading the cases present here, you may have some clues, but first you need to know what is murder. This is what many juries had to decide, a person has been killed, but were they murdered. Place yourself on the jury in each case and decide if the person is guilty.

WHAT IS MURDER?

The first source to check is *The Australian Magistrate* by John Hurbert Plunkett. Born in Ireland, Plunkett was appointed Solicitor-General of New South Wales in 1831 and by 1836 was Attorney-General. With a long career in the legal profession, he was responsible for many of the highly significant initiatives that changed the profile of colonial Australia.[2]

One of those initiatives was the compiling of a manual that provided a local magistrate with a succinct information to assist them in their duties. First published in 1835 as *The Australian Magistrate* it soon changed to *Plunkett's Australian Magistrate*, until 1903 when publication ceased.

Murder is the killing any person under the King's peace, with malice prepense or aforethought, either expressed or implied by law. Express malice is when one person kills another with a sedate, deliberate mind, and formed design; and the evidence of such malice must arise from external circumstances, discovering the inward intent, as lying in wait, antecedent menaces, former grudges, and concerted schemes to do the party some bodily harm.

Malice is implied by law in several cases; as if one voluntarily kills another without provocation; for no person that had not an abandoned heart would be guilty of such an act, and the law will in such case presume it to be malicious, and that he is a public enemy of mankind. Poisoning implies malice; and also, when an officer is killed in the execution of his duty, it is murder, and the law implies malice. It should be observed, as a general rule, that every homicide is presumed to be malicious, and, of course mounting to murder, until the contrary appears from the circumstances of alleviation, excuse, or justification; and it is incumbent upon the prisoner to make out such circumstances.

Murder must be committed by a person of sound memory and discretion; it cannot be committed by an Idiot, Lunatic, or infant, unless he shows a consciousness of doing wrong, and, of course, a discretion or discernment between good and evil.
It is a general rule that, to make the killing murder, the death must follow within a year and a day after the stroke or other cause of it. The Aboriginal Natives of the Colony are within "the King's Peace," and the unlawful killing of them is as much murder, as the killing of any other of the King's subjects.

RULES FOR THE MAGISTRATE OR CORONER

If the name of the deceased be known, it must be stated in the indictment, and be proved strictly in evidence, it is therefore essential that the Magistrate or Coroner in taking the Deposition, should ascertain what name he was known by in his life time.

The mode of death should be ascertained with as much care as possible in taking the Depositions; for if the species of death alleged in the indictment, be different from that proved in evidence the variance would be fatal to the case. It is necessary for the Coroner or Magistrate to probe well the immediate cause of death.

EXECUTION

9 Geo. IV. C31 s 4 – "That any person convicted of murder, shall be executed on the day next, but one, after that on which sentence shall be passed, unless it shall happen to Sunday, and in that case, on the Monday following; and the body of every murderer shall, after execution, be dissected or hung in chains, as to the Court shall seem meet. Sentence to be passed immediately after conviction, unless the Court see reasonable cause to postpone it."[3]

LAW AND ORDER

The New South Police Force as we know was not established until 1862. This provided central control with uniformity of staff across the State. Prior to this taking place the State was broken up into Police Districts with control by the local bench. Honorary magistrates appointed by the governor ran the local court and appointed persons to act as constables. These magistrates had no legal training and the standard and commitment to the position varied considerably. In some areas police magistrates were appointed and they had control of the local police force.

DEVELOPMENT OF TRIAL BY JURY

As there were developments in law and order there were gradual changes in court procedures and the availability of various courts. Here we are only interested to changes in criminal jurisdiction.

From 1788 Governor Phillip was authorised to establish a Court of Criminal Jurisdiction in which trials were heard before a Judge Advocate and a panel of six military officers. The NSW Act 1823 created the Legislative Council along with the Supreme Court and Courts of Quarter Sessions. Criminal cases heard in the Supreme Court were before a judge and seven military officers. Juries of 12 male civilians were used in criminal cases between 1824-28.

The Jury Trials Acts of 1832 and 1833 granted the accused person the right of trial by 12 citizens or seven military officers. A Juror had to be a male, aged between 21 and 60 years, natural-born subject of the King, income of at least £30 pa from real estate or personal estate of at least £300 pa. In 1837 the panel of seven military officers was removed[4].

POINTS FOR THE READER TO CONSIDER

In this volume there are details concerning 14 cases where the reader is invited to participate by placing themselves on the jury.

In each case I will play the role of judge. Anomalies in the evidence will be highlighted for your consideration. Keep in mind that the majority of the information came from newspapers of the era, some of the 'facts' may have been sensationalised to appeal to readers.

The cases start in the late 1830s. In some cases, the name of the deceased and murderer are unknown. The amount of information available varies from case to case, but I feel all are of interest. The book is not the definitive list of murder for that period; I am sure others will surface on the completion of this list.

LOCALITY OF THE MURDERS

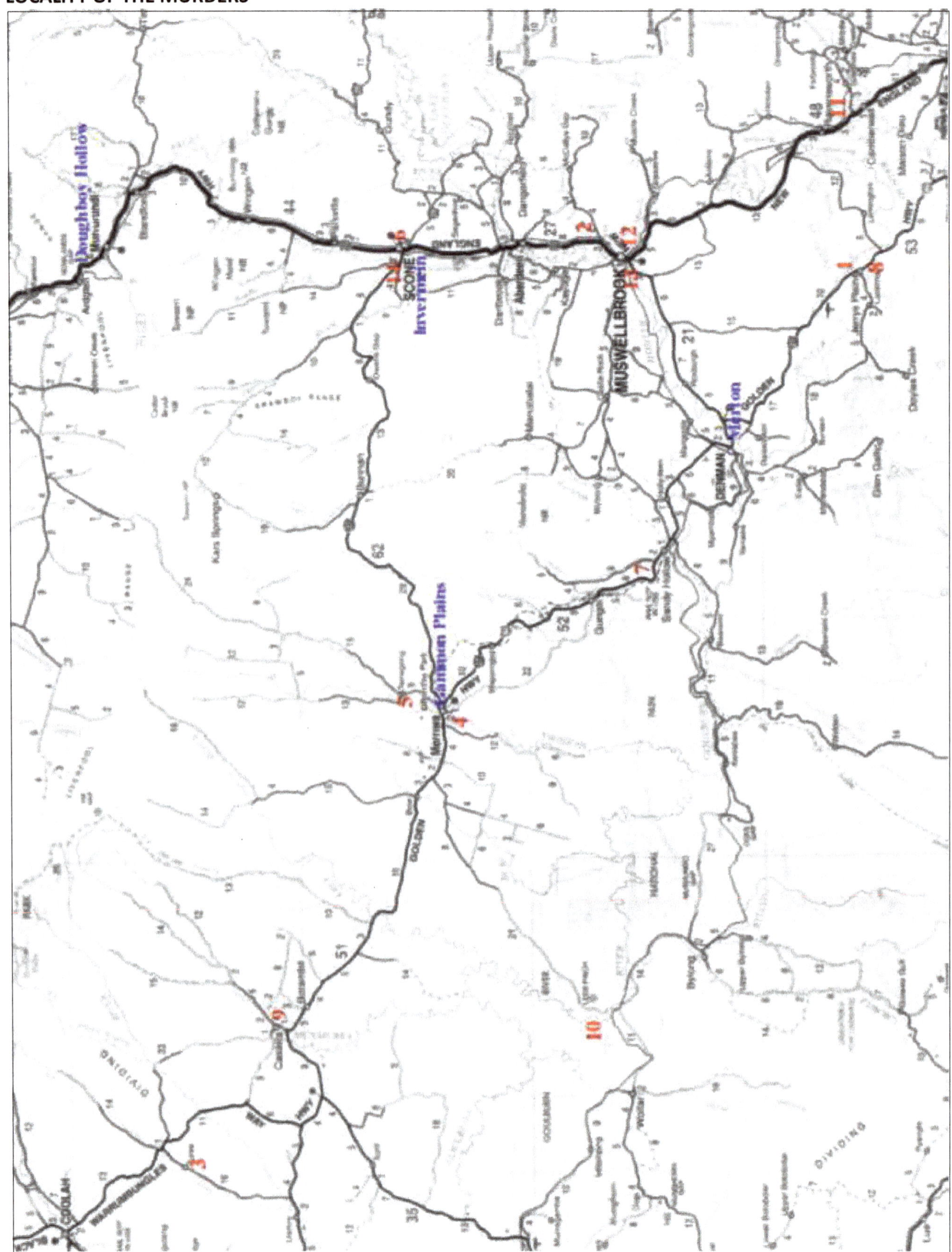

Modified from early NRMA road map. North is to the left. Red numbers align with each case. Localities in blue provide the original name of locality.

DETAILS OF THE CASES

CASE 1 - 1837 **JERRY'S PLAINS**

MICHAEL McSHANE **DECEASED VICTIM**

JAMES McKEEL **CHARGE WITH MURDER**

Sydney Monitor 14 August 1837. This report did not catch the excitement of the reporter for the *Sydney Monitor*. Very few details.

James McKeel, late of Merton, labourer was indicted for the wilful murder of Michael McShane, at Douglas farm near Jerry's Plains on 20th May, by beating and jumping on him.

It appeared in evidence that a constable named Fox was proceeding with two prisoners to the Plains [Patrick Plains, later Singleton] when they stopped at a hut on the road. One of the men was sent for two gallons of wine and the party became intoxicated.

The deceased provoked a fight between the prisoner and a man named Macguire who seemed unwilling; the deceased then struck McKeel and they wrestled together – the prisoner knocked the deceased down and afterwards jumped on his body, he was taken off and he ran away. The man died in about half an hour. The medical man was of opinion death had been caused by strangulation – the rest of the witnesses considered his death to be the result of the beating he had received.

The jury returned a verdict of guilty of manslaughter.

Sydney Monitor 23 August 1837
James McKeel, guilty of manslaughter, sentence of two years in an ironed gang.

What a party, two gallons of wine. Considering the period it was probably a light sentence.

CASE 2 - 1838 MUSWELLBROOK

JOHN BYDELL **DECEASED VICTIM, convict assigned to Lieut Col. Henry Dumaresq, St Heliers Station.**

MURDERER **UNKNOWN**

Persons involved

Archibald Little **Magistrate, settler at Cressfield**
John Goodwin **Surgeon, Invermein**

John Bydell's body was found on the morning of Wednesday, 14 March 1838 near the road leading from Muswellbrook to St Helier station. He had last been seen alive the evening of the previous day.

There seems to be some confusion regarding his name. Archibald Little, Magistrate of Invermein (Scone) investigated his death and reported to the Colonial Secretary that the deceased's name was George Boydler. The Colonial Secretary posted a reward in the *Government Gazette*, calling him George Boydle, yet John Goodwin, surgeon of Invermein who examined the body named him John Boydell.

The evidence available indicates that John/George was a convict who had been assigned to St Helier's station owned by Henry Dumeresq. At the time of his death the Superintendent was Mr Wightman. The station maintained a register of each convict in which were recorded details similar to that on each convict's indent. Also were recorded information regarding the behaviour, both good and bad of each person.

John Bydell – St Heliers Register

Ship	*Lord Mellville*
Sentence	Life
Date of sentence	27 March 1830
Year of arrival	22 September 1830
Native place	Stafford
Trade	Farmers man
Height	5' 5½"
Complexion	Dark ruddy
Hair	Brown
Eyes	Grey
Place of conviction	Warwick

General remarks: Found dead with his skull much fractured, March 14th 1838 near Sandy Creek Station. Enquiry held 15th by Dr A Little.

Although John had been on the station since 1830 there were no negative comments re his behaviour.
The Convict Indent provided further information: John could read, was able to plough, reap and shepherd. His crime was stealing eggs. He had one former conviction[5].

Archibald Little, report to the Colonial Secretary.

Sir, The, convict named in the margin [George Boydler] was found dead near this road leaving from Muscle Brook to St Heliers on the morning of Wednesday this 14th inst. – about 300 yards from the body a cheque ws found, torn into small pieces, which had been drawn by Mr Wiseman near Patrick Plains in favour of Mr Wightman the Superintendent at St Heliers and sent by the deceased.

As far as I have yet been able to ascertain the deceased was last seen at a sheep station of the late Col. Dumaresq & occupied by a Ticket of Leave man named Wiseman. He galloped off from Wiseman' door on Tuesday evening in the direction of St Heliers & must have met with his death very soon after, as the body was found at sun rise next morning only ¾ of a mile from Wiseman's hut. It was quite stiff & had the appearance of having been dead for a good many hours.

I proceeded to St Heliers on Thursday & examined several persons on Oath, but have not yet been able to ascertain how the deceased came by his death but strongly suspect that he must have been murdered. I enclose the

copy of a deposition made by Dr Goodwin who examined the body & be to recommend that such a reward as his Excellency may deem fit should be offered for the discovery of the perpetrator of the supposed murder in an early number of the Govt Gazette.
I have the honor to be, Sir, Your most obt. Servant, Archibald Little, JP.

Surgeon John Goodwin's report of his examination of the body provided to Archibald Little JP.

Before Archibald Little Esq JP.
Appeared John Goodwin Esquire & deposes that he is a Surgeon that was called on Wednesday the 14th Instant to examine the body of John Boydell who had been an assigned Servant of the late Col. Dumaresq at St Heliers & which body had been found dead that morning on the Estate nearly half way between Mr Wightman's house and the Hamlet of Muswell Brook.

I found the body lying on its face & left side, a few paces off the road, its left arm was folded under it, and the right was extended about an angle of 45° from the body, both hands were closed tho not firmly. On turning the body round, I found it was stiff and quite inflexible & from the incipient decomposition that was appearing I supposed that death must have taken place early on the proceeding evening.

After a very minute inspection I found no other injuries than a very severe fracture of the skull – fracture ten inches long. This fracture appeared to have been inflicted by a blow which had broken the left Parietal bone into three small portions, besides splitting this bone backwards until it reached the occipital bone, & forwards completely dividing the frontal bone over the frontal bone eminence, and superciliary ridge so that the frontal sinus on the left side of the head was completely divided.

The superficial integuments were but slightly abraded, having been defended by the hat, and only cut to the extent of half an inch over the compound fracture of the parietal bone, and to the same extent over the Nasal Fossa. The nasal bones having been also injured.

It did not appear to me that this fracture could have been produced by coming in contact or being brought in accidental collision with the trunk or brough of any tree near to the place where the body was found.

Neither were there stones nor any other substance that would render it probable that he met with his death from a mere accident. On the contrary the presumption appears to me to me very strong indeed that death in this case was produced by a long bludgeon or some other heavy blunt instrument, such as a bough of a tree, and which must have been applied with awful severity by the hand of man.

Sworn before me at Invermein 21 March 1838, Archibald Little JP
John Goodwin[6]

Colonial Secretary's Office.
Sydney, 3rd April, 1838.

FIFTY POUNDS REWARD;

OR,

A CONDITIONAL PARDON.

WHEREAS it has been represented to His Excellency the Governor, that GEORGE BOYDLE, assigned to the late Colonel Dumaresq, was found dead near the road leading from Muswell Brook to St. Heliers, on the morning of Wednesday, the 14th ultimo, and is supposed to have been barbarously murdered by some person or persons unknown:—Notice is hereby given, that a Reward of Fifty Pounds will be paid to any free person or persons, except the actual perpetrator, who shall give such information as may lead to the apprehension and conviction of the party by whom the said murder was committed; or if the informant be a prisoner of the Crown, application will be made to HER MAJESTY for the allowance to him of a Conditional Pardon.

So, was John Bydell murdered? No record has been found of anyone being charged.

Points of interest:

- Archibald Little 'examined several persons on Oath' but he does not provide information as to who they were.
- What was Bydell's role on St Heliers?
- Why was Bydell visiting Wiseman?
- Was Wiseman one of the persons examined?
- If so, what did he have to say under oath?
- What is the significance of the torn-up cheque?
- Were there trees in the area that the deceased may have ridden into?
- Where was Bydell's horse found?

What happened to Bydell's body. Goodwin mentioned that it was starting to decompose, perhaps it was interred where found. In 1838, the closest consecrated burial ground was at Kayuga and at least one convict from St Heliers is known to have been buried there; that place is a possibility.

Justice Burton (State Library of NSW).

CASE 3 – 1838 **TUREE**

JOHN JONES **DECEASED VICTIM, station owner, Turee**

EDWARD TUFTS[2] **ACCUSED OF MURDER, TL holder employed by late John Jones.**

PERSONS FOR THE PROSECUTION
James Burgess **overseer to late John Jones, Turee**
John Wilson **blacksmith assigned to late John Jones, Turee**
Alexander Bushby **settler and magistrate, Cassilis**
Mark Howell **surgeon**

PERSONS FOR THE DEFENCE
Edward Tufts **TL holder, Turee**

Background

This case occurred at Turee Station, on the banks of Talbragar River, being part of the Macquarie catchment. It is situated to the north west of Cassilis, which, at the time was the closest court and police district. It is included in this account of murders, though technically it is outside the Hunter, as it has a connection to Case No.10

The deceased, John Jones arrived in the Colony as a free man per *Nile*, on 14 December 1801, accompanied by his wife Mary and daughters Mary Ann (aged three years) and Susannah (one year). Early the following year he was granted 100 acres at Toongabbie. Later he moved to the Windsor area which became his base for the next 20 years. During that period, he undertook a number of ventures such as settler, builder and brewer. His wife Mary died during this period and he married Ann Palfrey nee Bartlett, she was 30 years of age and had a two year old son, Joseph.

John Jones became involved in the building of St Mathew's at Windsor, acting as superintendent. Governor Macquarie was so pleased with Jones' work he granted him 500 acres at Bathurst. The exact date of his move to Bathurst is unknown, but he has four more children with Ann; John, Alfred, Adolphus and Reuben.

In 1835, John Jones applied to purchase Portions 1 and 2, Parish Turee, an area of 2620 acres, he later added other portions which increased his holding to 8833 acres. Jones utilised his building skills to organise a fine sandstone homestead. By 1837 there were 19 assigned persons and 21 free working on the property.

On 21 October 1837 shearing was in progress at Turee Station and it was standard practice to wash sheep before shearing. This was a daunting task for the persons involved as they stood for hours in the water with the sheep ensuring that dirt was removed. To provide some comfort and encouragement the men were issued rum during the work and at the end of the day. On this particular day, Edward Tufts attacked John Jones with sheep shears. Jones was wounded in the thigh and groin, six days later he was dead[8].

Tufts was charged with the murder of John Jones and his case came up on Wednesday, 13 February 1838 at the Supreme Court in Sydney before Mr Justice Burton and a Military Jury.

We will now adjourn to the newspaper reports of the day for an account of the trial. The accuracy and detail in the reports vary depending on the reporter.

Sydney Gazette 22 February 1838.
Sydney, Supreme Criminal Court, before Mr Justice Burton and a Military Jury.
Edward Tufts was indicted for the wilful murder of John Jones, by stabbing him in the groin with a pair of sheep-shears, at Turee, on 21st October.

James Burgess, overseer to the late Mr Jones at Turee, in the county of Bligh – Mr Jones died on 27th October about 3 o'clock. I recollect the Saturday night before his death; we had been sheep-washing, Mr Jones attended it. Mr Jones, Tufts, and me came home together, Tufts was a ticket of leave man employed by Mr Jones, to whom I believe he had been assigned. Mr Jones told me to give the men a glass of grog each as they had worked hard and washed upwards of eight hundred wethers. I gave them a dram glass full of rum each. [A small glass]. Some of the shepherds came in about eight o'clock.

---

[2] There are varying spellings for his surname.

Jones gave every shepherd who reared a lamb for every ewe a £5 as a premium. Thurston, one of the shepherds, received £5, and craved very hard for some spirits. Mrs Jones said she could not give it as she had not enough for the sheep shearing. Mr Jones said she had better give a little, and I believe Thurston got some spirits, but I do not know how much. I afterwards saw Thurston with some spirits in a pint pot. William Lilly, another shepherd, was called in and received £3 10s. He went out and I afterwards went into the kitchen. I then went up to Tufts hut, Lilly and me had a quarrel, Mr Jones heard the noise and came up and told me it was no place for me and I went to my own room in a place joining the house. I had been asleep a little while when I heard Tufts calling Mr Jones a robber and other names.

Tufts was not tipsy; I got up, put on my clothes, and went to my door, and heard him call him [Jones] all the thieves, robbers, and vagabonds he could set his tongue to, and said he had robbed him of four hundred sheep; John Wilson, the blacksmith, came by, and I said if Mr. Jones will put up with this he will put up with anything, the blacksmith went to Tufts' door and Tufts asked him if he was going to take a pill for Jones; the blacksmith went round to the left and I went to my master and said if you put up with this you will put up with anything, and Mr. Jones said that he did not mean to put up with it and would settle with him another day.

Mr. Jones came out and sung out to Tufts, I will settle with you another day; Tufts came from his hut and appeared to walk to the left, and then walked past me towards Jones who was on my right; I then heard Jones say, Tufts, you have murdered me, oh Ann Jones I am a murdered man. I cannot say how near he went to Mr. Jones; I did not see him nearer than two rods because there was a kind of parting; I saw Tufts within about half a rod when he went round a corner. When Jones said he was murdered I could not see him; Tufts made a run towards the blacksmiths' shop followed by Jones, who went a step or two and then turned to his own door; I then saw Jones throw the shears down saying those are the shears that murdered me.

When Tufts passed me I did not see anything in his hand; these are the shears, when I saw them there was blood near the point and the point was bent as it is now; Tufts went towards his own hut and said, I have settled the old sweep at last, he repeated it several times; this was about two minutes after he came from Mr. Jones. When I first saw Tufts after Mr. Jones called out, he was running from the house; Mr. Jones was wounded in the side of his groin and his thigh; a doctor was sent for.

Mr. Howell came; this was on Saturday, the 21st October, and Mr. Jones died on the following Friday; a few minutes after my master was in the room I apprehended Tufts, he made no resistance; when he was lying on the floor in the kitchen. He said he was very sorry that the old man must die, but he knew the shears touched the bone. These are the trousers the deceased had on; I saw these holes they correspond with the place where the wounds were; (the trousers were completely saturated with blood) the deceased never walked nor got out of his bed afterwards.

Cross-examined – I was drinking no where that night; I only took one glass of spirits; I was not drinking, I did not swear I was; it was in the prisoner's hut I took the glass of rum; I was not drunk before I went to bed; I do not know how many bottles of rum were drunk; I only saw some in a pint pot; I never heard the prisoner make any threats towards Mr. Jones; the prisoner was expecting that the deceased would give him some sheep after shearing, and he was depending upon his signing a petition for his emancipation in October, he had mentioned it that day. The deceased was a passionate man at times; the prisoner's shirt was not torn that night that I knew of, but I lent him a clean shirt to go to Court in. Tufts kept a woman, who asked me to lend him a shirt; I have drawn rum from Mrs. Jones in part of my wages; it was the custom to supply the free servants with rum, the convict servants could not get it; the free servants could only get a small supply; I never knew the free servants sell it to the convicts; I do not recollect that the prisoner paid a pound for a bottle of rum for him and me to take to Tonga; the woman that lived with the prisoner was a free woman; there was a woman living with Shepherd at a station about six miles off.

By the Court – These women were not married then, one of them is married since; they were both fond of drink, the prisoner's woman particularly, she was always craving for rum; a man named David Gill used to bring rum on to the farm sometimes, I do not know whether he had a license; there was a place about three or four miles off where rum could be got; whilst the men were shearing and washing they had had three bottles between eleven of them; the prisoner had some of it; it was served out by me at four different times; they were in the water about five hours, and had one glass going in, two while they were in, and one coming out; I did not go into the water but had the same rum as they had; I do not know whether the prisoner's woman was off the farm that day; I saw no strange men there that night.

John Wilson – I was blacksmith at Turee; I was assigned to Mr. Jones; I was at the sheep-washing; after coming home I went to the men's hut, and when coming up again at night about nine o'clock I heard a voice; the sheep washing was over about three o'clock, I had a little to drink after I got home, I dare say about three glasses, which were given to me by a free man named Thornton. I heard the prisoner having some words with my master; I went to the prisoner's hut and he told me to go away to my hut. Mr. Jones came up and asked me what I was doing; I said I knew I had no business there and went towards the overseer's hut; about an hour after this I heard some high words, the prisoner was against his own hut; I heard the prisoner saying something about some sheep.

I was about six yards from them; I was not tipsy; they were talking angrily, the prisoner called my master names; I do not recollect what names; on my oath I do not know what names; the master was walking in front of his own house, I did not hear him say anything; the prisoner went into the hut and came out again immediately; I do not know whether he had anything on his head; he went as if going towards the back of the building, and then turned short and came to the house, he passed me within two or three yards, and almost directly I heard Mr. Jones cry out that he was murdered, and I saw the prisoner run away; I ran towards my master, who said, catch him, and I went a few yards after the prisoner and then turned back to my master who had got into his bedroom and was down on his hands and knees.

Cross-examined – I had three glasses of rum that night; I was not drunk, and did not swear that I was; I did not see anybody drunk; I drank the rum in the kitchen; the deceased was a violent, passionate man sometimes; the deceased had not drank anything that night that I know of; rum was sold on the farm; when it was there any of the men could get it; I don't suppose they could get all they liked; I have bought rum, a pint was the most I could get at one time; I have no doubt that I have got more than one pint in one day; I do not recollect who paid for it; I got it from Miss Christie, and I suppose I must have paid her for it; I swear I paid for none at that last sheep shearing; I do not know that Mrs. Jones sent for ten gallons for sale unbeknown to Mr. Jones; I have fetched rum to the blacksmith's shop for men not belonging to the establishment, but it is a long time ago; I did not see the prisoner's shirt torn that night.

Alexander Busby, Esq., J. P. – I took this deposition from the late Mr. Jones on the 23d of October; the prisoner was present, charged with stabbing his master; it was taken at Turee, the residence of Mr. Jones; it was taken down by me as Mr. Jones gave it, read over to him, and signed by him in my presence. The prisoner asked Mr. Jones if he thought he entertained any malice towards him, and Mr. Jones replied that from the expressions used by the prisoner he thought he had.

Cross-examined – I think that Burgess admitted before me he had been drinking, Wilson did the same, by my impression is that they said they were sober enough to know what had occurred. Mr. Jones was reputed to be a violent man; it was reported that rum was sold in the establishment; the deceased's application for assigned servants was refused at the September session, the assessors did not consider him a proper person to have servants; I did not tell the prisoner I considered him the victim of the illegal sale of spirits.

By the Court. – I am a sheep-holder; as a matter of opinion, I should say it is not necessary to issue spirits to men at the sheep shearing, but it is generally done; as regards the health of the men, my opinion is that it is not necessary; it may be considered necessary as it is the custom. I believe there are not wanting instances of sheep being washed without; Mr. Charles Blaxland, it is reported, has done so; I have done so myself when I happened to be without spirits, - the ration of tea and sugar was increased as a substitute.

I believe, to a certain extent, it is the custom to supply servants with spirit; there is a great thirst among free labourers at that season of the year for spirits, and if they are not liberally supplied they will not work, and persons who are dependent on them are obliged to comply with them; about three years ago I hired free men, and the uproar on the farm in consequence was great; their demands were unreasonable, but there was no refusing them, and the whole establishment was in confusion; I have managed to do without them since; I think the practice of supplying servants with spirits for pay does prevail at that season of the year – I mean as remuneration for extra labour, not for money, but I have heard for money; I should say a free man would not be satisfied with a pint of spirits per day; I found it necessary to leave off supplying spirits.
By the Attorney-General – My opinions are founded on extensive experience among large establishments; I have about forty convict servants, if they were taken from me, I should be obliged to hire free men and comply with their demands; in cases of this kind I prefer convict to free labour; I have heard that free men refuse to hire where spirits are not allowed.

Burgess recalled, and examined by the prisoner – I heard that some time before this Mr. Jones drank a glass of sugar-of-lead water instead of rum; that day Mr. Jones said he was much better than he had been for years, in consequence of leaving off drinking; Mr. Jones mentioned making the mistake at the water hole.

By the jury – Mr. Jones was a very kind master.

Mr. Mark Howell – I am a surgeon, and took my degree at Lincoln's Inn, in 1833; this is the only document I have with me; (a certificate of having attended Bartholemew's Hospital) I have not been drinking to-day. I will not swear to it; I drank a little water when I washed my teeth;

I saw Mr. Jones on the morning of the 22nd of October about one o'clock; he was wounded in the groin and thigh; the wound in the groin was about five inches in length; there was about a yard of intestines protruding; Mr. Jones said, doctor, I am no more; the artery was wounded; I tied the artery up; the wound was the most dangerous one I ever saw; I dressed it and put him to bed; he was in great pain when I first came, but he obtained relief by the dressing; I remained there until Wednesday when he died; I was in the house all the time.

After death I examined the body; the intestines were very much wounded; there was a wound in the groin an inch and a half in extent, and in the thigh about an inch; the body was perfectly healthy in all respect except mortification in the intestines produced by external causes; the wound in the thigh and groin were the first cause; the wounds that I saw might be produced by these sheep shears.

Cross-examined – I heard Mr. Jones drank some sugar of lead water; that had nothing to do with producing the mortification.

The witness having given his evidence in a very flippant, disrespectful, vulgar, incoherent manner, the Judge called Mr. Busby, who said the witness appears to me to be intoxicated; he is generally remarkably respectful; I never saw him in this way before.

The Attorney General said, that under these circumstances he would recall Mr. Busby – I saw all the symptoms of a very severe wound in Mr. Jones's groin; the dressing was removed at Mr. Jones's request, and he then pointed the wounds out to me; he said he was suffering greatly, and I should think he must be; there was a great enlargement and discoloration of the parts.

Mr. Jones spoke of his death as being to take place immediately; I expected it. I believe this to be prisoner's hand-writing; it was given to me either by Mr. or Mrs. Jones. (Letter read from the prisoner to the deceased before his death, requesting him to be as lenient as possible.)

His Honor ordered Mr. Howell to be confined in Sydney Gaol six months, for giving evidence in a state of intoxication.

This was the case for the crown.

The prisoner's defence was – That he had taken so much rum that he could not recollect what had happened; he bore no malice to the deceased, and in fact his death was a great injury to him.

His Honor said that in all cases of murder it is necessary to prove, firstly, that the death of the person said to have been murdered has taken place; secondly, that he died by the means laid in the information; thirdly, that he died by the hands of the prisoner, and fourthly, that the prisoner did it of malice.

In consequence of the manner in which Mr. Howell had behaved, the Jury must throw his evidence out of their consideration, and must say whether, from the facts sworn to by the other witnesses, they believed his death was caused by the means stated in the information. It had been proved that he was in good health before he was stabbed, and he took to his bed immediately after and did not get up again, and died in a few days. If the Jury believed that the act was committed under the circumstances stated in evidence, he was bound to tell them that in law it was a case of murder. The prisoner had stated that he had no malice towards the deceased, but if a case of homicide was proved the law presumed malice, unless circumstances arose in the course of the case to show that it was a less crime, and in looking through this case he did not see any such circumstances; on the contrary, the deadly instrument with which the deed was committed, and the part of the body in which the wound was inflicted, were facts from which the law presumed malice. As for the prisoner's being drunk, if persons voluntarily get intoxicated, they must answer for what they do when they get sober.

The Jury retired about a quarter of an hour, and returned a verdict of Guilty. Remanded.

Australian 16 February 1838
Edward Tufts, convicted of the murder of his master, the late Mr John Jones of Turee, during a fit of phrensy[3] resulting from intoxication received sentence of death. His Honor remarking that the awful situation of the prisoner at the bar was mainly attributed to the indiscreet act of his master, in suffering the indiscriminate use of intoxicating liquors among his convict servants.
Sydney Monitor 28 February 1838
Yesterday morning [Tuesday] the sentence of death passed on Edward Tufts, convicted of the murder of his master, Mr Jones of Turee, [commonly called Gentleman Jones[9]] was carried into effect. Tufts was attended to the place of execution by the Rev Mr Cowper and appeared penitent. When on the scaffold he uttered a few words, cautioning the people to take warning by his fate, and to refrain from drunkenness.

Background to Edward Tufts

Edward Tufts was born around 1803 in London and was 19 years of age when he was tried at the Old Bailey on 5 December 1821 and received a sentence of transportation for life. From Newgate Prison he was sent to the *Bellerophon*, a prison hulk moored on the Thames. The prison Ship Register records his offence as being 'stealing wearing apparel from the person'. He had a short stay on the *Bellerophon* for on 29 March 1822 he joined the *Guildford* for NSW.

Tufts' Convict Indent indicates he could read and write, occupation shoemaker, 5' 3½" in height, pale, pox-marked complexion, brown hair and grey eyes. He was assigned to Thomas Hawkins of Bathurst. At the time of the 1825 Muster he is still in Bathurst, but assigned to John Jones. The 1828 Census shows Tufts still with Jones and a house servant. By 1837, Jones has moved to Turee, Tufts is there with him but now holds a TL for the district of Cassilis.

Thoughts concerning the case

- The altercation between Tufts and Jones took place at night, unless there was a full moon it would be difficult to see what was happening.
- Tufts called Jones a thief, robber and vagabond plus accused Jones of robbing him of 400 sheep. What had Jones done that caused Tufts to use such harsh words, [Tufts was a TL and perhaps Jones was paying him with sheep rather than cash].
- Jones told Burgess and Tufts that he was not going to put up with Tufts behaviour and 'I will settle with you another day'.
- What did Jones intend to do to Tufts?
- According to Burgess, Tufts had left the scene and it was Jones who threw the shears down claiming that 'they were the shears that murdered me'.
- Tufts was expecting to be given more sheep after shearing and that Jones would sign a petition that would allow Tufts to obtain a conditional pardon.
- Tufts had been a convict for 15 years and with Jones for 12 and there are no known records of any misdemeanours in that period.
- There was a history of excessive use of rum on the station without a license. It is difficult to determine if anyone was sober on the night of the incident.
- At least two persons claimed that Jones was 'a violent man'. Alexander Bushby, magistrate, did not hold Jones or his establishment in very high regard. Another magistrate happened to stay at Jones' property one night. He found Jones in 'a state of frenzied drunkenness roaming from hut to hut until two in the morning'. Ferris found that such 'occurrences were frequent; Jones was remarkable as a boxer, fight his men and terrorise his wife and family'.
- Jones was in the habit of drinking sugar-of-lead water[4].
- Mark Howell, surgeon was an unreliable witness, and his evidence was struck out.
- The accused, Edward Tufts had no one to defend him except himself.

---

[3] **Phren'sy**, *noun* s as z. [supra.] Madness; delirium, or that partial madness which manifests itself in wild and erratic sallies of the imagination.
[4] **Sugar-of-lead** is lead acetate, is soluble in water and provides a sweet taste. Had been used since the Roman era for sweetening wine. Highly toxic and leads to lead poisoning which has a number of symptoms including mood disorders and difficulty with memory.

- Jones' wounds were in the leg and groin, an unusual place to stab someone if the intention was to kill them.

You, the reader will have to make up your own mind as to murder or manslaughter, but I feel that today with a competent defence legal team, Tufts would have received a reduced sentence or found not guilty.

Grave of John Jones, Turee Station. It is believed that his son, also John is buried long side John snr.

CASE 4 – 1839 GAMMON PLAINS (MERRIWA)

CONSTABLE FOX DECEASED VICTIM

JOHN HOBSON (OPOSSUM JACK), ACCUSED MURDERER

John Hobson was one of the most notorious bushrangers in New South Wales in the 1830s and 1840s, but today his name is almost unknown. He was a farm boy from Sheffield. On 21 January 1828 he was tried at Doncaster for stealing handkerchiefs and received a sentence of transportation for seven years. Though only 17 years of age, he had two prior convictions. He arrived in Sydney, November 1829 and was assigned to George Blaxland at Brush Farm[10].

By 1833 he was at Wollun, near Merton on the farm of Gregory Blaxland. On 14 March he absconded, but apprehended was the following month and sent to the No. 3 iron gang at Newcastle. The Iron Gang managed to contain him until December 1837 when he absconded and returned to the Merton district and committed a number of depredations on the settlers. The government offered a reward of £10 for his capture[11].

Hobson with others continued to harass settlers with impunity and there were calls for the government to send a stronger Mounted Police force. In May 1839 Hobson added murder to his list of crimes.

Edward Denny Day, police magistrate at Muswellbrook informed the Colonial Secretary of the murder:

> I have the honour to report for the information of His Excellency, the Governor that Constable Fox of the Cassilis district was murdered on Thursday last at a station of Mr W C Wentworth at Cream of Tarter Creek, near Gammon Plains in the county of Brisbane by the notorious John Hobson, alias Opossum Jack who at the time was accompanied by two other runaway convicts named Knight and Wilson. The latter of whom fired at and wounded a man named Bayliss who was assisting Fox in pursuit of the bushrangers. Bayliss, I am happy to say escaped with his life, but Fox was killed on the spot[12].

The government offered a reward of £45 for the capture of Hobson and £10 each for Francis Knight and John Wilson. Later the reward was increased to £50 or a free pardon and passage to England. Hobson was described at 4' 11", sallow complexion, light brown hair and grey eyes. Knight, 5' 6", ruddy complexion, brown hair and light hazel eyes while Wilson was 4' 9¾", fair ruddy and freckled complexion, red hair and brown eyes[13].

It is unknown what happened to John Hobson, he did not end up on the gallows nor was he shot by a trooper's bullet. There were indications that he was killed by James Martin, one of his associates, but that may not be correct as various newspapers reported he had been active in the Mudgee area. It is believed he died on the Liverpool Plains at the hands of Aboriginals.

Almost no information has been located concerning Constable Fox, not even his burial place.

Major Nunn - see Case 5.

CASE 5 - 1840 **GAMMON PLAINS (MERRIWA)**

JOHN JOHNSTON **DECEASED VICTIM**

JAMES MARTIN	**ACCUSED MURDERER**
JAMES MASON	**indicted for aiding and abetting James Martin**
JOHN WALKER	**indicted for aiding and abetting James Martin**
JAMES HOWARD	**indicted as accessories after the fact**
ROBERT RAWSON	**indicted as accessories after the fact**

PERSONS FOR THE PROSECUTION

Henry Pelham Dutton,	**settler, Terragong, Gammon Plains**
Thomas Giever	**convict assigned to Mr Bettington**
Lieut Richard Talbot Sayers	**80th Regt, Mounted Police**
Arthur Blaxland	**settler, Gammon Plains**
Dr Michael McCarthy	**Gammon Plains**

PERSON FOR THE DEFENCE

James Martin	**convict**
Green	**convict**

This is an unusual case. Normally newspapers carry reports of the murder, hunt for killers, arrests and news on the transfer of the perpetrators to Sydney, then the report of the trial and finally reports of the execution if the accused were found guilty. John Johnston died on 24 March 1840 and the first news regarding a possible murder at Gammon Plains was the report covering the start of the trial on 7 November 1840.

After a diligent search utilising Trove, a small paragraph in the *Australasian Chronicle*, 18 August 1840 provided the answer.

> The Attorney General stated that with regard to the four convicts from Gammon Plains, charged with murder, although they had been some months in custody, yet through the difficulty that had arises between Major Nunn and Lieut Sayers he had only received the depositions about ten days ago, and therefore was unable to proceed to trial. Postponed till next term of the court.

Major Nunn and Lieut Sayers had a tumultuous relationship. Both were part of the 80th Regiment which was stationed in NSW from 1837 to 1844. Part of the regiment was utilised to form the NSW Mounted Police which included Nunn and Sayers. Their relationship came to a pinnacle during the investigation of the attack on Dutton's homestead at Gammon Plains and the killing of a servant. Nunn made nine charges against Sayers which resulted in a general court martial. The court found Sayers guilty of one charge and part of another and returned him back to duty with no penalties. The Court Martial held up the trial of the persons arrested by Sayers in relationship to the case concerning the death of John Johnston of Gammon Plains. Sayers' depositions concerning the case were incomplete when he was arrested and Nunn 'misplaced' the case notes that Sayers had provided to him.

Start of the trial of four convicts from Gammon Plains.
The majority of the information regarding the trial is from the *Sydney Herald*, 9 November 1840. Text in [ ] is additional information from the *Sydney Monitor* 9 November 1840.

James Martin, late of Gammon, was indicted for the wilful murder of one John Johnston, at Gammon on the 24th of March last; James Mason and John Walker were indicted for aiding and abetting the murder; and James Howard and Robert Rawson were indicted as accessories after the fact, by harbouring the prisoners after the felony had been committed.

The Attorney-General commenced the proceedings by giving an outline of the case, and stated, that two of the prisoners were assigned to Mr Blaxland, while the others were the assigned servants of Mr Bettington; and called:

Mr Henry Pelham Dutton, who deposed – I am a settler, in March last I lived on Gammon Plains; on the 24th of that month an attack was made on my house by some men, about half an hour after sundown. Mrs Dillon and three of my children were in the bedroom; I was going through the passage to the hall when I heard a loud crash, and was surprised to be met by two men with masks on. One of them presented a gun at me and threatened to blow out my brains if I did not go to the upper end of the room; I asked them if they intended to use any unnecessary violence, and they said they did not; they then brought Mrs Dutton and the children into the same room with three female servants, and two children belonging to one of the females. Shortly after two of my men servants were brought in; I saw four men at different times, all of them in smock frocks; they had masks on which covered the whole of their heads to the shoulders; one of them searched my pockets, but found nothing. About three quarters of an hour after they came, I heard two shots fired in the hall, on which the man who was standing over me sprang out of the French windows by which they entered; soon after another of the men came from the hall evidently expecting to be attacked, and also passed out of the window.

Soon after this one of my servants named Burrows came in with a gun in his hand and told Mrs Dutton not to be afraid as they were all there. [Witness went out into the kitchen and found the deceased supported by Lee, one of the witness's servants. Deceased was a ticket of leave holder] I was then shown the deceased who was wounded on the right side of the head which was bleeding very profusely, he died about three quarters of an hour afterwards. One of them who stood over us appeared to be the shortest of the four; another of them appeared to be very active on his feet, they spoke frequently and appeared to be Englishmen. They used a very threatening manner to me about my firearms. I told them they were in possession of the house and could satisfy themselves. My little son, five years old told them how many guns and pistols I had in the possession of the carpenter, Johnstone, the deceased. The window was secured in a temporary way by a bolt as it had been only placed there two days before, it could not be pushed open without violence, there were a great many panes of glass broken. I missed a good deal of my wearing apparel and a number of Mrs Dutton's trinkets.

Martin asked the witness in what part of the house Johnstone was shot. Witness – I should suppose it was in a little parlour from the marks of the blood. When I entered the room, it was filled with the smoke of gunpowder, I could not see what took place in the hall.

Thomas Giever[5] deposed – I am an Irishman from the County of Mayo. I have been four years in the colony come Christmas, I came in the *Bengal Merchant,* I came from Sheerness, I was a pedlar and tried at Newcastle for stealing a watch; I was sent here from the assize for seven years; I have been punished four times, twice for losing sheep, one for leaving my station without a pass and once for refusing to carry the rations fifteen miles, my punishments were fifty, one hundred, twenty five and fifty lashes. I was assigned to Mr Bettington three weeks after I arrived; I was last at Boggybrine, a station about three miles from Mr Dutton's and eight miles from the head station; Mason and I took the bush on the 9th March and got over the Liverpool Range, Walker and Howard were at the same station; Mason, Green and I did one robbery while Mason, Green and Dailly did another. Green was assigned to Mr Blaxland and Dailly to Mr Bettington.

James Martin, James Mason and James Walker and I did the robbery at Mr Dutton's on the 24th March, we were then stopping with Howard and did not determine on whether we would rob Mr Dutton or Dr Macartney until Walker joined us on the Spring Creek, when Mason and Walker joined us we determined to go to Mr Dutton's and set out about an hour and a half before sundown, the only arms that we had were a cut down musket and a fowling piece and all the ammunition we had was in the guns. We had all masks on made of cloth, two of which were made of new print and the other two were made of an old shirt with holes cut in them to see through. When we went to Mr Dutton's, we stood for a little to see that all was quiet, after which Martin burst in the door and I followed him.

Mr Dutton then came in and Martin seized him and told me to put him up in the corner of the room and to shoot him if he moved. I had the cut down musket. Walker had the other gun and the remaining two had sticks which they had cut before we went into the house. The others then went and brought Mrs Dutton and the children and the female servants. After about half an hour I saw one of Mr Dutton's servants enter the room with a pistol in each hand and told Walker to stand, on which he rose the fowling piece and told him to stand, when the man fired and wounded Walker on the breast, on which Martin seized the pistol out of the servant's hand and shot him in the head.

I immediately ran out and made for Martin's station and found him there with Green and Henry Beverson. Martin told me he had left Walker at his own station and about half an hour after Martin overhauled the plunder. There were a good number of things, three or four sovereigns and some orders, two pair of Wellington boots, a number of gold rings, an ink stand, a cruet stand and several other things, Martin had charge of the things. He told me and Mason that the best thing we could do was to leave the station for some days, we then went to several stations, but only stopped for refreshment.

[5] Several different spellings for his surname.

One of the stations I have heard belonged to Mr Jones, we returned to Martin's about ten days after and found he had moved to another. We went to him and he told us he would get us some money and passes; that we might pass for immigrants. Martin and Beverson drew us our rations regularly. Beverson is dead, I struck him with a tomahawk, which he had struck me with.

On the Wednesday morning, they brought us beef and milk, he poured out the milk and it was so bitter I could not drink it. Marton and Mason tasted it and sent Beverson for more milk; he was away about twenty minutes. When he returned, he took the tomahawk in his hand, saying he would go and look for an opossum and just as I was going to eat, I received a severe blow on the back of the head which stunned me. I got two other strokes on the front of the head, the skin on the back of my head and part of the flesh were hanging down. I ran five or six yards and fell hurting my shin, I got up and ran again when Beverson pursued me about half a mile with the tomahawk. I cast off my jacket and waistcoat and ran till I got to the road between Bow Plains and Cockabill, when I fell down in consequence of loss of blood. I lost the use of my limbs, on which Martin seized me and Beverson came up and was going to strike me again, but Martin would not allow him, as it was too near the road. They then took hold of my arms and lead me back. I begged hard for my life, particularly of Martin, but he told me it was no use and said he wanted none of my preaching. He said when I was apprehended in a day or two, I would tell of his shooting Mr Dutton's man and they could not spare me. I then asked him to shoot me, but he refused to do that as the report would make an alarm.

I then asked him to give me the laudanum bottle I knew him to have, and I would drink it sooner than be again struck by the tomahawk. Beverson then went and got the two-quart kettle and the laudanum bottle and poured in about an inch and a half into the lid of the kettle. I was not willing to drink it, but they told me if I refused, they would be worse to me. I then drank about half a glass full of the laudanum at two gulps and they took me and set me under a large tree and sat down about a quarter of an hour with me and seeing that I was not going to sleep, they then gave me the rest of it and about a quarter of an hour after they made a bed for me with an opossum cloak and told me I must lie down. I refused; they told me I must do so as the more I refused the worse punishment they would put me to.

I laid down and Martin said he would go and look after Beverson 's sheep and he went away. About ten minutes after I said to Beverson I would sleep better if had my boots off, when taking them off I sprang to the tomahawk and seized it; he sprang at me, I got it and he and me had a wrestle, we fell, when I got clear and struck him two blows on the temple with the tomahawk which knocked him down, I then made my way to one of Mr Leslie's stations about seven miles off. After I had gone off, I saw him rise and lean against a box sapling. When making my way to Mr Leslie's I threw up the laudanum in froth, when I got there, I drank tea and water and throw it off my stomach. I was then sent to the head station. Martin told me he intended to kill me because I had seen him shoot Mr Dutton's man. Mason was sitting beside me when I was first struck. Martin told me that Walker has been wounded in the breast. I gave information to the constables and on the Saturday while I and the constables were looking for Mason, we saw the body of Beverson about a quarter of a mile from where I struck him. I afterwards showed Mr Sayers of the Mounted Police where I had been struck by Beverson and Mr Sayers by the help of Green recovered part of the stolen property. I have not seen Walker till then, till I saw him in Sydney. Howard was at the same station with me. Rawson was assigned to Mr Bettington. Mason went for Walker on the night of the robbery.

Cross examined by Martin: You supplied us with firearms on the day of Mr Dutton's robbery, you lent us the arms before, when we went to rob one of Mr Jones' stations, you also lent us the arms when we robbed Mrs Howards, and also when we robbed Mr Wentworth's station. There was no water in the laudanum when I took the first dose. I swear that I saw you shoot and murder Mr Dutton's man. I swear that I saw you on the night after the robbery, I never told anyone that Dailly supplied me with the firearms.

Joseph Brenan who was objected to by Martin, as having been in court during the examination of the last witness. Brenan denied on oath that he had been in court and deposed that he was overseer to Mr Dutton and on the night of the robbery was about half a mile off, when being told of the attack, I, the deceased and two other of Mr Dutton's servant, got armed and made arrangements for taking bushrangers, when deceased left the party and got in before the others and I heard two shots fired; I ran up and saw a man making off; he called out shoot the b-d, I fired at him, when he dropped a bundle, which we found contained some property belonging to Mr Dutton and was covered with blood. I only saw two of the bushrangers, we recovered the pistols principally through voluntary information given by Walker. When we went into the house, we found the family all in confusion and the deceased was walking about deranged with his brains hanging out, he died about three quarters of an hour afterwards. After Walker mentioned the pistol, I asked him where it was and he told me it was forgotten by Roper alias Martin, where Mr Dutton's black boy found it, the pistols were loaded with gunpowder and duck shot. After the bushrangers went away, we found two strange hats in the parlour, one of which was produced in court.

Johnson[6] only called for his master and wanted to speak to him. I saw the shot extracted from Johnstone's head; it was similar to that with which the pistol was loaded.

Cross examined by Martin: I do not know what room of the house Johnstone was shot.

Lieut [Richard Talbot] Sayers of the 80th Regiment who had command of the mounted police in the district of Gammon at the time of the robbery got information of the murder and robbery about the 27th of the month and immediately turned out his party, when they kept beating about for information. When the approver[7] Gievers gave information that induced him to take the party into custody and found that the statement of Gievers was corroborated by the locality of the place where Beverson had been murdered, on searching he found tracks of the opossum cloak having spread on it and a piece of damper and crumbs of bread as if some person had been eating there. The marks of the cloak were by the grass having been beaten down the reason Lieut Sayers went so particularly about the information given by Grievers was that it was of such an extraordinary character that they could scarcely believe. Approver then took the party to a new made grave about half a mile off, where there was a large pool of blood and where Beverson was buried. Sayers was surprised on looking at the distance between the Curryjong (sic) tree where the scuffle took place between Gievers and Beverson and was of opinion that the latter had not met his death under the tree. He found traces under the tree of a scuffle having taken place between white men, the traces consisted of marks of the feet of white men, afterwards took Howard and Rawson into custody for harbouring and for being accessories after the fact, when they admitted having taken care of Walker's sheep on the night of the robbery and murder at Mr Dutton's. On the whole Mr Sayers collaborated the statement made by Gievers, he also proved the finding of the cut musket and the fowling piece in such a way as to commit the prisoners the circumstances they found concealed in the vicinity of the stations where the prisoners were assigned, he also subsequently discovered that the fowling piece had been stolen from Mr Jones' station some time previous to Mr Dutton's robbery. It was also proved by Mr Sayers that on the day after the robbery Martin was seen with a white shirt on.

Mr Arthur Blaxland, a magistrate of the Territory, proved [John] Walker's making a voluntary confession after being in custody at the Gammon lock-up, after his wound had been examined and dressed by Dr McCarthy, he told Walker that it was a bad case for him, but if he would confess all, the Magistrates would consider his case. The prisoner then paused for some time and then made the confession. The prisoner Walker after being told that he was one of the parties at the robbery, and that it would be better to confess, said to the Magistrates, yes, I was one of them, and I know I shall be hanged for it.

Dr McCarthy proved that the wounds on Walker's breast and arms were gunshot wounds with shot such as the pistol had been charged with when Johnstone fired it.

[Dr Macartney deposed: He was a surgeon practicing at Gammon Plains, he inspected the body of Johnston on 26th March, he had known him before, the wound was in his head, and his death was caused by a gunshot wound. Witness took about fifty duck-shot out of the brain. Re-examined by the Attorney General: Examined Gievers – found three recent wounds on the head which could not be made by himself. Also examined Beverson – there were incised wounds on the head, one of which was broken in. Would be impossible for a man to walk with such wounds.]

James Martin, in defence, stated that the case had been made up between Green and Gievers, to save themselves as had not been in any way connected with the robbery, the other three prisoners stated that they had nothing to say, and Rawson denied that he had any knowledge of the robbery and the murder until he was told of it when he was getting rations. Martin stated that he subpoenaed his overseer, at the time of the murder, in order to prove that at the time of the murder he had a sore foot and that it was impossible for him to travel nine or ten miles to do the robbery, he also stated that as the approvers Green and Gievers had been in custody six or seven months, they had plenty of time in order to get the story concocted, he also insinuated that the account given before the Court had varied materially from that given by the witnesses before the Magistrates. The deposition was then read at the request of Martin.

From that of **Green** it appeared that Martin had been in the bush with Opossum Jack, whom it was generally supposed Martin had put aside to the knife, tinder-box and pistols of Opossum Jack had been seen in the possession of Martin, not since then, Opossum Jack had never been seen since he was also accused by several of the Government men of the neighbourhood of having killed Opossum Jack on which he being then in liquor, fell a crying.

---

[6] Number of spellings in newspaper reports.

[7] Approver, Old English law, a participant in or accomplice to a crime being tried who gives evidence for the prosecution.

The Chief Justice, in putting the case to the jury stated that the case was one of considerable importance, not only from the interest which this case had excited out of doors, on account of the place in which the murder and robbery had been committed, as being in a lonesome part of the Colony, where there was but slight means of protecting the lives of the inhabitants, but also because it involved the lives of three of the prisoners. He also adverted to the law of the case, as respects those present when the murder was committed; and also adverted to the necessity that exists for admitting approvers the whole of whose evidence it was as necessary to corroborate, but merely to see that the gaps and chasms in it were filled up and that the whole body of evidence was consistent in all its parts and called the attention of the jury to the cross-examination of Mr Dutton in which the prisoner Martin showed such knowledge of the circumstances that had occurred at the house of Mr Dutton, as could only have been obtained by his being present at the murder. He also pointed out to the jury the close corroboration which Green testimony had received from Mr Sayers, Mr Dutton and several other unimpeached witnesses; and stated that the jury was first to make up their minds respecting Martin, Mason and Walker, and if they were guilty, then they were to enquire whether Howard and Rawson had been guilty of harbouring and abetting them; at the same time, he considered the evidence against the latter as of a slight description. After summing up the prisoner Martin said, the way in which he had come to the knowledge of the bushrangers having threated the life of Mr Chiesly, by saying at Dutton's that they would have his life and would swim in his blood, was, that he heard the prisoner Walker tell it to the Magistrates; that was also the way in which he became acquainted with the fact coarse language had been used by the bushrangers.

The Jury retired for about ten minutes, and returned a verdict of wilful murder against Martin, Mason and Walker, and a verdict of not guilty against Rawson and Howard. The Jury, before returning their verdicts wished to be informed what Mr Dutton had to say in favour of the prisoner Walker; when Mr Dutton said that Walker had shown great civility to Mrs Dutton, the children, and the females not having ill-used them in any way, and when he bailed them up, he behaved with becoming respect to them.

His Honor said it would not affect the prisoner's guilt.

Proclamation being made, his Honor gave a feeling and impressive address commenting on the mass of crime which the trial had brought into view as connected with Martin, which he regarded as being unparalleled in the history of the colony, as there was good reason for believing that he had frequently imbrued his hands in the blood of his fellow creatures. From the details given on this trial there was strong reasons for believing that his old confederate Opossum Jack, who had been the scourge and terror of the Colony, had been destroyed by him. It was also clearly proved that he had shot the deceased man, Johnston, while his attempts to deprive his accomplice, Gievers of life was such as to strike terror to the hearts of everyone who heard the given by that individual. His Honor also said that the blood of Mason and Walker, the youth who stood with him at the bar, was also chargeable on his head; and after having admonished each of them to prepare for a future state, passed sentence of death on all of them in the usual form. The prisoners heard their sentence unmoved, and appeared unaffected by what had been said to them.

EXECUTION OF THE BUSHRANGERS

Sydney Herald, Wednesday, 9 December 1840

Three criminals expiated their crimes on the scaffold in front of Sydney gaol, yesterday morning. James Martin and John Mason (along with John Walker) were convicted at the late sittings of the Criminal Court, of a robbery and murder in the residence of Henry Pelham Dutton, Esq. Gammon Plains. Walker, for having prevented violence to the person of Mrs Dutton, has had his sentence commuted.

William Newman, the other malefactor, had also been sentenced to death for murder. Our readers may remember that during the trial of Martin and his associates, a series of murders and other atrocious crimes were deposed to, the details of which were given in the *Herald* at the time, of which history has scarcely any parallel. To this circumstance is probably owing the unusual excitement to witness the execution. The works and high ground behind the gaol, commanding a view of the horrid spectacle, were crowded, as also was the gaol-yard, where a strong military guard had been posted. In addition to the usual paraphernalia of death usual on such occasions at home were three coffins places under the scaffold. In front of the drop five cushions were arranged – three for the murderers and two for the clergymen. Exactly at nine o'clock Martin made his appearance; he walked with a firm step, followed by his wretched associates in crime. The three knelt devoutly on the cushions provided for them, and the other cushions were occupied by the Rev Mr Cowper and the Rev Mr Elder. All three joined with apparent fervency and devotion in this solemn act of duty, the responses being repeated in a firm tone by Martin. The service being concluded, Martin was the first to rise. He looked around for a moment, and ascended the platform with a firm step, placing himself near one of the ropes fixed to the fatal beam. His demeaner evicted neither bravado or timidity, but the conduct of a man who knew that his life was justly forfeited for a long course of profligacy and villainy. The caps having been placed on the heads of the wretched men, all three prayed with fervency and feeling.

EXECUTION OF MURDERERS AND BUSHRANGERS
Australian, Thursday, 10 December 1840. This newspaper provided another description of the execution along with a summary of the case which makes it easier to understand.

Three wretched men underwent the last penalty of the law on Tuesday morning, in the rear of the Sydney Gaol. Two of the malefactors had been, at the recent sittings of the Criminal Court, convicted on the clearest evidence, of the triple crime of bushranging, burglary and murder; and we are no advocates of capital punishment, yet when every post brings us frightful details of the excesses committed upon person and property by parties 'out in the bush', we are inclined to think that, in the case of at least one of these atrocious offenders, it was wise in the Executive to put in force the fatal terrors of the law.

James Martin had been the leader of a desperate gang of ruffians in the neighbourhood of the Hunter's River. He supplied them with fire-arms, regulated their movements, kept a store for stolen property and managed the sale of it. He also, as was proved on his trial in the Criminal Court, on the 7th November, and from other established facts, had been in the habit of murdering systematically and in cold blood, such of his accomplices as fell under his displeasure. The circumstances which came out in evidence were most extraordinary and such as to call forth the following remarks from the learned Chief Justice in passing sentence. 'He could not help observing that the mass of crime which the trial had brought to light in regard to Martin was, he believed, even in the history of this penal colony, unprecedented. There was every reason to suppose that he had frequently imbrued his hands in the blood of his fellow creatures, and that amongst other victims might be enumerated Opossum Jack, his old confederate, who had long been the scourge and terror of the country, and above all, the cold blooded and deliberate manner in which he had attempted to take the life of Gievers, his accomplice, who had that day been admitted Queen's evidence, was such as to strike terror into the heart of every individual who had listened to the horrid details'.

The facts thus adverted to by the learned Judge were these: - Martin, with four of his gang, went disguised in masks, to the house of Mr H P Dutton, Gammon Plains.

While in the act of plundering the house John Johnston, a servant of Mr Dutton's rushed in with a loaded pistol in each hand, one of which he fired off and wounded John Walker, one of the robbers. Martin then snatched the other pistol from Johnston's hand and discharged the contents at his head. The brave man who had endeavoured to defend his master, died in a few hours, and the bushrangers made off with much valuable property. The gang then under Martin's directions, dispersed for a short time to avoid detection. Gievers, one of them, returned in a fortnight and claimed his share of the booty, but Martin resolved to put him out of the way and by the assistance of a man of the name of Henry Beverson, compelled him to drink a quantity of laudanum. Gievers, after undergoing a series of cruelties, wounded Beverson in the temporary absence of Martin (who had left Gievers, as he said to 'die easy') and made his escape; his stomach having rejected the laudanum. Gievers then gave information to the head of the mounted police of the district, who hunted out and apprehended Martin along with James Manson and John Walker. In searching the district, the mounted police discovered a grave, recently dug, near which was a pool of blood. In that grave was found the body of Henry Beverson, the man who had assisted Martin to murder Gievers, and had been wounded by Grievers at the time of his escape, and the natural inference is that Beverson had been murdered and buried by Martin.

At the trial, four men were indicted along with the leader of the gang, two of whom were acquitted, but James Mason and John Walker were found guilty of having been present at the robbery of Mr Dutton's house and the murder of poor Johnston. Walker was recommended to mercy by the jury, for having prevented personal violence to Mrs Dutton, and for the manner in which he behaved to the children and female servants. That recommendation has been attended to and the life of Walker will be preserved, that he may linger it out in an iron gang; but John Mason was executed on Tuesday morning along with the atrocious Martin. Also, William Newman, for the murder of Henry Hodgson, at Singleton, Patrick Plains, by stabbing him with a knife, suffered at the same time.

It is probably owing to the peculiar circumstances attending the career and character of Martin, that the anxiety to witness the execution was so great. By eight o'clock, the rock and high ground behind the gaol, commanding a view of the horrid tragedy, were crowded; and before nine, a great concourse of spectators was admitted through the wicket of the gaol in George Street. There was the scaffold, under which had been placed three coffins, destined to receive the bodies of the malefactors. After a pause of a few minutes, a rather tall, dark-visioned dark-haired good-looking man (Martin), dressed in white trousers and jacket, made his appearance at the door leading from the condemned cells. He was born in 1804, and was consequently thirty-six years of age; and arrived in 1827. William Newman, a good-looking young man, twenty-eight years of age, was followed by James Manson, aged nineteen, with expressive feature. The clergymen in attendance were the Rev Mr Cowper and the Rev Elder.

These gentlemen knelt in front of the culprits, and the usual service on such occasion was read by the Rev Mr Cowper. Martin held up his head all the time, and responded in a very audible and firm voice. The youth, Mason, seemed to listen with devout attention, and Newman often joined in the service.

This solemn part of the tragic scene concluded, Martin rose. He looked, far an instant, at the coffins under the scaffold and heaved a sigh so loud as almost amounted to a groan, and a tremor shook his frame. It was but momentary – for he was the first to ascend the ladder, which he did with firmness and without assistance, as did also the other men. Three ropes were dangling from the transverse beam of the gallows, near to one of which Martin placed himself. It seemed now as if every fibre in his frame shook with emotion; but he again rallied. The executioner approached to adjust the ropes. This duty over, he placed on the head of each a white cap. The clergymen then advanced, and held a few minutes converse with the wretched men.

Newman seemed to communicate something with great earnestness; Mason was nearly all the time engaged in frequent prayer; and Martin said a few words (if we may judge from his manner) in a dogged tone. The executioner then drew over their faces, and tied with a string, the white caps – the bolt was withdrawn – and the men launched into eternity. The fall of the rope was greater than we witnessed at an execution in England, and the deaths of the malefactors more sudden. Martin, however, in a short time after life seemed to be extinct, and when the bodies of his wretched companions had ceased to move, was dreadfully convulsed. It was, altogether, a solemn scene.

So, dear reader, member of the jury, what are your thoughts?

I as the judge believe you made the correct decision regarding James Martin; a more dangerous villain has not crossed my Bench in all my time as a judge. John Walker, you recommended for mercy due to his courteous treatment of the Dutton family. You found him guilty of the charge, therefore, by law I must impose the death sentence and leave the decision regarding his life to a higher authority.

James Mason, you found to be guilty of aiding and abetting Martin in the murder of James Burrows. I believe you made the correct decision. Mason, while only a young man (about 18 years of age) had started on a career of crime at an early age and arrived in this colony with a sentence of seven years transportation. He was young and perhaps in awe or fear of Martin, but aiding and abetting is a legal concept where someone is held liable for assisting another person in committing a crime, even if they did not directly commit the act themselves.

If the reader is interested in further information a more comprehensive account of this case, I suggest they obtain a copy of the following from the Merriwa Historical Society:

Andrews, E, 2007, Murder at *Terragong*, published by the author.

Edward Denny Day, Police Magistrate.

CASE 6 – 1840 ST AUBINS, SCONE

John Graham	**DECEASED VICTIM, storekeeper to Thomas Dangar**
JOHN SHEA	**CONVICT, ACCUSED MURDERER**
JOHN MARSHALL	**Convict, indicted for aiding and abetting John Shea**
JAMES EVERETT	**Convict, indicted for aiding and abetting John Shea**
EDWARD DAVIS	**Convict, indicted for aiding and abetting John Shea**
ROBERT CHITTY	**Convict, indicted for aiding and abetting John Shea**
RICHARD GLANBY	**Convict, indicted for aiding and abetting John Shea**

PERSONS FOR THE PROSECUTION
Attorney General assisted by Mr Therry

Edward Denny Day	**Police Magistrate, Maitland, formerly Muswellbrook**
James Jewshaw	**saddler employed by Thomas Dangar, Scone**
Mrs Chivers	**wife of George Chivers, publican of St Aubins, Scone**
William Day	**cook for Mr Chivers**
John Patterson	**settler near Scone**
James Norval	**servant to John Patterson**
Richard South	**publican near Murrurundi**
Isaac Hague	**surgeon, Scone**
John Nowland	**constable, Muswellbrook**

PERSONS FOR THE DEFENCE
Mr Purefoy for Davis (the rest were undefended)

This is a very interesting case, which is a small part of the story of the 'Jewboy gang of Edward Davis. If you are interested in the full story of this gang of bushrangers then you should read *An Organised Banditti, The Story behind the 'Jewboy' Bushranger Gang* by Colin Roope and Patricia Gregson. An excellent read providing valuable information on convicts, and life in general during the early 1840s within the Hunter Valley. The case is also interesting in that a number of Sydney newspapers carried the story of the chase up the valley by Edward Denny Day, the capture of the gang, trial and subsequent execution of some members. In comparing the reports, it becomes obvious that to rely on a single newspaper for coverage of the events could be perilous. The following story is a compilation of the various newspaper reports.

CAPTURE OF THE BUSHRANGERS
The Sydney Gazette and New South Wales Advertiser 31st December 1840.

The news of the capture of the notorious band of bushrangers at the Hunter having reached Sydney at a late hour on Monday last, precluded us from giving any further than a mere announcement of their being taken. We have now great pleasure in laying before our readers as nearly as we can gather the whole particulars of the case.

On Sunday night, about nine o'clock, Mr Day, Police Magistrate, received intelligence that the bushrangers were at Muswellbrook, and that they had threatened to attack the settlers there. *The Sydney Herald* reported that on Sunday, 20th instant the bushrangers had visited the station of Sir Francis Forbes (Skellatar) about three miles from Muswellbrook and bailed up the persons there, they did not depart until nearly sundown. On the bushrangers leaving the station a ticket of leave man by the name of Jones lost no time in reporting the matter to Mr Day. Mr Day immediately called upon some of the neighbouring gentlemen, and some ticket of leave men, and about seven o'clock next morning they departed in pursuit of the gang. *The Sydney Herald* lists the men as Mr Edward White, (brother of Mr James White Edinglassie), Mr R C Dangar the Chief Constable, John Nolan, Peter Daw, Martin Kelly, William Evans, William Walker (the five latter are ticket of leave holders), Martin Donohue (assigned servant) and a black boy.
By this time the gang amounting to eleven men, and had been committing deprivations on every side. They had robbed Turanville, the residence of William Dangar Esq., about four o'clock in the morning, and at six o'clock they were at Mr Thomas Dangar's stores, where the murder of Mr Graham took place, the particulars of which we have given in a former publication. Having committed this robbery and murder, the miscreants deliberately mounted their horses and proceeded towards the Page, where they robbed Mr Atkinson's Inn and the store of Mr Rundle.

Mr Day, and his party were in hot pursuit. On reaching Scone, Day and party went to the Court House. The police along with two magistrates were sitting and there were a number of settlers about the place. It would be assumed that they would be interested in the capture of the bushrangers, but no exertion was being made nor had any notice been given to out-lying settlers. Day was also unable to obtain a fresh horse from one of the settlers, then at the Court.

At this stage, Mr E Warland, Robert Evans, John Teely (both ticket of leave holders) and one of the border police joined the party.

The falling of a heavy rain and the rapid rate at which the ruffians travelled, prevented their being overtaken until they arrived at Doughboy Hollow (Ardglen) over the Liverpool Range. Mr Day and party had fortunately paused in Murrurundi to reload their firearms due to the damp inclement weather. Dr Gill joined the party at the Page. When Mr Day's party came up to them, they immediately took to the trees. Davis the Jew, fired two shots at Mr Day which, however we are glad to say had no effect. Davis was then severely wounded in the shoulder, and after five shots having been fired was captured. After eighteen shots had been fired by the bushrangers, and two of the others wounded, they laid down their arms and surrendered. Their capture was effected exactly 11 hours after the murder of Mr Graham. The ruffians were then handcuffed and taken to the lock-up in Scone.

The Sydney Herald reported that on Day's party arriving at Doughboy Hollow they observed some drays encamped along the creek. The party proceeded towards the drays and soon after saw some horses, and directly came in view of the bushrangers. It was now six o'clock. Mr Day and his party dashed on at full gallop, cheering as they went; the bushrangers stood to their arms and took to the trees. Robert Chitty was first taken; he fired one shot and was not allowed time to reload and was thus secured. Davis and Marshall were next secured. Davis fired four shots, in two he of which he took deliberate aim at Mr Day. Marshall fired two shots. Shea and Ruggy ascended a hill overlooking the combat, and from there fired ten shots. The bushrangers in all fired eighteen shots during the capture, fortunately not one of which took effect. In less than five minutes, five of the bushrangers were secured. It has not been ascertained how many shots Day's party fired, but Mr Day wounded Davis in the shoulder (he also had a ball through his trousers) while Shea was wounded in the calf.
The next morning Day and party set off to escort the captured men to the lock-up at Scone while five men and two black boys set off after two men who had escaped during the fight. After eight miles, they came upon Glanville (Glanby) who admitted to firing one shot during the fight. We are sorry to state that one of the miscreants effected his escape.

When, within thirteen miles of Scone they met a party forwarded by Mr Robertson (Police Magistrate, Scone) to assist in escorting them, as he considered, no doubt, according to his usual clear way of thinking, that a party who after riding fifty miles in eleven hours, and were able to capture them, would not be able to take care of them. Mr Day was not impressed with the conduct of Mr Robertson and on the following day refused to sit on the Bench with him. Mr Robertson was unable to commit the bushrangers from the Scone Bench, although the murder was witnessed and there were witnesses in attendance to prove it. They were then committed from the Muswellbrook Bench. The bushrangers were found with seven horses, nine double guns and rifles, a great many pistols, several watches, sixty to seventy pounds in money and a many other articles.

They were committed for trial on Wednesday. So secure in themselves had these ruffians got, that they wore flags and ribbons during the last day of their career, and had the impudence to send the police word to bring the dead cart with them when they came in pursuit. It would be impossible to bestow a more that just quantity of eulogy on Mr Day for his gallant and manly conduct in the whole of this affair, for to his courage and determination in the whole mainly to be attributed. The gentlemen who accompanied him are likewise deserving of the highest praise; their names are Messrs Edward White, Richard Dangar, Edward Warland, and John Hill. Two ticket of leave men named Evans and Daws, acquitted themselves in the most gallant manner; in fact, the whole party deserve the highest credit.

The ruffians arrived in Sydney about midnight on Monday, and the manner in which they did so was terrible. They came along George Street, strongly guarded and heavily ironed; instead of looking dejected or penitent, they were all laughing, singing and cracking jokes, as merrily as if they were enjoying themselves in a public house. We never in our lives saw such a fearful example of human depravity. We hope that no time will be lost in bringing them to trial, and there is no doubt but they will be found guilty, we hope their execution will not be delayed. It is almost a crime to suffer such ruffians to exist. We would not however, run the risk of taking them to the scene of their crimes, but have them executed in Sydney.

A committee has been appointed to present Mr Day, with a piece of plate. Upwards of £100 was subscribed at the Upper Hunter, and a very large sum is expected, as the settlers feel very grateful to Mr Day, for his exertions.

SUPREME COURT – CRIMINAL SIDE

BEFORE CHIEF JUSTICE DOWLING AND JURY

The Sydney Gazette and New South Wales Advertiser 27th February 1841

John Shea convict, was indicted for the wilful murder of John Graham by shooting him at St Aubins[8], on the 21st December last. John Marshall, James Everett, Edward Davis alias Wilkinson, Robert Chitty and Richard Glanby (Glanville) convicts, were indicted for being present aiding and abetting in the same. A second count stated the murder to have been perpetrated by some person unknown, and charging the prisoners with being accessory to the crime.

Mr Purefoy appeared on behalf of Davis and the Attorney General was assisted by Mr Therry.

The Attorney General, in opening the case, stated that all the prisoners at the bar were charged with the murder of a young gentleman of the name of Graham. All the prisoners were convicts assigned to separate masters, and that they had been sent to the Colony to be punished for their bad conduct. That the indulgence of being assigned was extended to them through the leniency of the Government, a leniency they had no right to expect, and what was only known to the law in modern times (1840s). That the prisoners had put no value upon the kindness that was shewn them, but, instead, had kept all the northern parts of the colony in terror and confusion, and had shown themselves incorrigible. He thought it expedient to trace a part of their career. He found them at Brisbane Waters, at which place they were joined by Glanville and from what took place there it was clear that persons of their class could not move through the country unless assigned men harboured them and others friendly to them in the various districts, who thus made a profit by the plundering carried on. Glanville was comfortably situated, but he took a step that in this country is considered to lead to the gallows. He took to the bush and joined the other desperate characters, scouring the country with an audacity never equalled. Decorating themselves ribbons, changing horses as it suited them, they at length found their way into Scone. On Sunday, 20th December, they were seen in the immediate vicinity of Scone, bent on their unhallowed designs; next day they entered the village well mounted. Glanville and some of his companions rode into the store yard belonging to Mr Thomas Dangar others went to Chivers' public house, on the opposite side of the road. The person they were charged as having murdered John Graham, who was storekeeper to Mr Dangar. It was reported there some time before, that this party were out, and from various circumstances they at once knew who they were.

Mr Graham in consequence, took up a pistol, it is not known whether he fired it, should he have done so or not made no difference, for when a party of men leave their services and go about the country armed, they are beyond the pale of the law. Mr Graham, in directing his steps to the lock-up, was, in rounding a corner, fired on more than once, but only received one shot, it was in the spine, and proved almost instantaneously fatal.

While this was going on, the party was plundering Messrs Chivers' and Dangar's. The shots had been heard; Marshall came running up, stating that "the fellow was settled." Someone asked if he was dead, to which Marshall replied, he was all right; it appeared that they had mistaken Graham for Dangar's son, for one of them asked if it was him that was shot. Marshall answered, "never mind, he fired a shot at us and we fired one at him."

The Attorney General then said that the Jury would of course take the law of the case from the Judge, that common sense would lead everyone to the conclusion that men who went about robbing all over the country, armed to the teeth, would never have been so armed unless they intended using them when thwarted in their designs.

After recapitulating their career thus far, he (the Attorney General) said that Mr Day, Police Magistrate, having heard of the outrages they had committed, and being within a day's ride of them, in the most gallant and praiseworthy manner (though not in his own district) summoned all the ticket of leave men he could muster, and started in pursuit. They followed the bushrangers, closely traced them by the robberies they were committing from place to place, at length he came up to them, when all the prisoners fired on him, and his party, though fortunately without any effect, having boasted afterwards of firing fourteen shots.

[8]Now part of Scone, NSW.

Davis, who was a kind of ringleader, fired twice at Mr Day, deliberately, knowing that their only chance of escape lay in taking his life, but they were, through the interposition of Providence, foiled. Mr Day wounded Davis. When the bushrangers' ammunition was all exhausted, they were taken prisoner with the exception of two, one of whom was captured next day, and the other he doubted not was by this time apprehended, or at least shortly would be.

The indictment in the first instance charges Shea with murdering Graham as he had told Mr Day so, though others of the party were wishing to take the credit of having sent a human being out of the world with all his sins upon his head. Shea persisted that he was the person; but in the eyes of the law, it did not signify – all the aiders and abettors being equally guilty. The result of this case he hoped, would be further proof, that the first step to the gallows, was for a convict to become a bushranger.

Mr Edward Denny Day deposed that he was a Police Magistrate at Maitland, and formerly at Muswellbrook, he was at the latter place on private business; having received information he mustered a party of men, went in pursuit, and at length came up at Doughboy Hollow with Davis' party. They were round a dray, some of their horses were tethered; they galloped in amongst them, and after a good deal of firing, succeeded in capturing five of them; Davis was one of them. He had fired at him repeatedly, which he returned; the skirmish did not last five minutes when they were all except Glanville captured. He held out no inducement to make them confess to anything though he kept his party all night awake. Davis said that he was always opposed to the shedding of blood. Marshall remarked that he would shoot any man that fired at him, and that Graham was a foolish young man, and could expect nothing better by his firing at a band of armed men. He said he would shoot his father if he fired at him. They all said that up to that morning they had done nothing to endanger their lives. They found scattered about eleven guns, twenty pistols, besides some trinkets and about £80 in cash found upon their persons.

James Jewshaw (Jewshan) examined – Said he was a saddler in the employ of Mr Thomas Dangar; knew John Graham the storekeeper; he was about 24 years of age; saw him on the morning of the 21st December; saw a man come into the yard on horseback, and about a minute afterwards observed a number of horsemen pass the gate; said to a man that was working with him, "these are bushranger." Put down his work and went out by the back way to acquaint the police. Graham went by the road; he went by the bush road. Saw Mr Graham run, then walk, heard two shots fired and saw Mr G fall; he had a pistol with him. When he went up to him, Graham said, "Saddler, I am shot through, I am a dead man." At this time, he saw a man on horseback, who said, "come back here or I shall blow your brains out."

Went back and heard him tell his comrades, as the man was shot, there was no time for delay. He was so frightened that he could not recognise any of the prisoners. They remained about twenty minutes at Mr Dangar's, saw seven men leave Mr Chivers' house. Mr and Mrs Dangar and son were at home. As soon as the bushrangers went away, he ran up to Graham who died in about ten minutes afterwards.

Mrs Chivers said her husband kept a public house in Scone; on the morning of the 21st December, saw three persons on horseback ride up to Mr Dangar's whom she took to be gentlemen, but when she saw pistols, and ribbons on one of their hats, thought they were bushrangers. When she went to the door to ascertain who they were, one of them accosted her, and told her that he knew she had plenty of money and he must have it. She then got the cash box, put out of the window to him. It contained £30 in £1 notes, a £2 note, a half sovereign and £20 in silver. She told him there were orders in the box; these he said were of no use to him. She heard several shots fired and saw Mr Graham taken home dead from a gunshot wound near the back. On her cross-examination, she stated that Davis told her not to be afraid and was very civil to her all the time.

William Day deposed – He was cook at Mr Chivers' on the 21st December; on that day recollects two or three men having come to the place. One of them, Everett collared him and bailed him up. Swore that if witness resisted, they would shoot him as well as the other man they bailed up. Saw a shot fired along the road about 100 yards from Mr Dangar's house; it was at Mr Graham; he was running from Mr Dangar's. The person who shot him was 20 yards from him, saw Graham fall.

Several others witnesses were called to the box, viz, Mr Joseph Chivers, Mr Thomas Dangar, Mrs Sarah Dangar and son, Mr Isaac Hague &c, all of whom deposed to the main facts of the indictment.

William Jones, a labouring man, stated that he was at work in the bush, about two miles from Muswellbrook; I saw the six prisoners on the 20th December last; there was a lot of horses at the Creek, did not see anyone till I was turning back, and he then called on me to come forward, he said to the other man behind in the creek that he had one prisoner; asked him what he wanted of me; he told me to go down into the creek; that man was Chitty, I then saw four others sitting down, Marshall and Everett came up to me, and took some provisions I had, they were all armed and had pack horses. This was the night previous to Graham's death. This witness, on leaving the dock, was addressed by Everett in these words, "I hope you may be the next that will be shot, and all such bloody dogs."

Mr John Patterson a settler, residing near Scone, identified all the prisoners coming to his house and stealing a horse from him, they were all armed, some with and others without hats, one man at least had blue ribbons[9], this is a distance of four miles from where Mr Graham was murdered.

James Norval identified the six prisoners as being in company along with a seventh, who came to his master's house, and calling for refreshments, desired him to hold their horses; witness was directed to give notice of the approach of anyone. One man said, go in, we will shoot a man in a minute – we have shot one already. This man, witness believed to be Davis; witness was bailed up. Davis had stopped at the house once or twice before to take dinner.

Richard South, a publican residing within twenty-five miles of Scone, saw all the prisoners in company; they bailed up witness and his family up, broke up some firearms he had; Marshall said he would deal with me before he went away; I had been stopped a short while before on the road. Davis and Shea were in company at that time, and they took from me my horse; they remained at the house one hour.

Isaac Hague, Esq. surgeon examined the body of deceased Mr Graham death was occasioned by the infliction of a musket ball passing through the cavity on the left side of the chest, and lodging in the muscles. The ball entered at the back, within two inches of the spine, death must have ensured a few minutes after.

John Nowland, constable, was one of Mr Day's party. Shea fired and so did Everett that he noticed; the party fired sixteen or seventeen shots at us; we captured five that night and Glanby the next morning was overtaken and begged for mercy; this was the case for the prosecution.[14]

Mr Purefoy appeared for the prisoner Davis and argued that there was no evidence to show that his client was aiding and abetting in the murder of Graham.

The Attorney General contested that he, Davis was aiding and abetting at the time the murder was committed by standing sentry over the parties who were bailed up in Mr Chivers' bar. He then reminded the Jury, that it was a principle of British justice, that if persons went out to commit a robbery, and there was a murder perpetrated by any of those who went out to commit the first (that unless the others prove they had no participation in the second); they were all, in the eyes of the law, legally guilty as accomplices.

His Honour then summed up, addressing the Jury in a most powerful speech. Afterwards the Jury retired, and after an hour and a half's consultation, came into court and delivered a verdict of guilty against all the prisoners.

After silence was proclaimed, his Honour, having placed on his head the black cap, proceeded to pass sentence of death on the prisoners. The feeling and impressive address of his Honour on this occasion, was well calculated to affect the heart of the most indifferent; but these ruffians appeared as unconcerned as if the whole affair was a mere ceremony and not of the slightest consideration to them.

Davis who all along anticipated an acquittal, was seen to shed tears on the verdict being announced. All the prisoners were conveyed to gaol in quarter of an hour after the trial was over.

Leading to the execution

The Australian 13th March 1841

The Hunter's River bushrangers, six in number, who are under sentence of execution, were warned on Thursday evening last, by the Sheriff, not to entertain the smallest hope that the order for their execution on Tuesday morning next would neither be deferred nor rescinded. The Executive Council, which sat on Saturday last, relative to the case, on receiving the Judge's report, were unanimously of the opinion that the extreme sentence of the law ought to be carried into effect upon each individual culprit.

Towards Davis public sympathy seems to be a good deal excited. The culprits have been attended for several days past by the ministers of their respective persuasions. Their execution will take place in the Sydney Gaol, at the usual hour, on Tuesday morning next. (Since writing the above we learn that a very urgent appeal has been made

[9] Bushrangers often wore ribbons on their hats, may have been symbolism with the Ribbonmen of Ireland.

to the Executive, particularly on behalf of Davis. The friends of this unhappy criminal relied mainly on the point adduced in evidence, that he was averse to the shedding of blood; but the Council, in having their attention addressed to the point immediately refer to the evidence of Mr Day, who swore that Davis placed a musket in the fork of a tree and took deliberate aim at him twice to take his life. We hate public executions; but the question arises, whether the public justice of the country would be satisfied by foregoing the Judge's sentence. For the present we forego answer.

There were three reports of the execution. All have been quoted as each portrays a slightly different view of the execution.

Execution

The Sydney Herald, Wednesday, 17th March 1841

The gang of ruffians recently convicted in the Supreme Court, of bushranging and murder, and for several months previously had infested the Hunter's River district (even extending their depredations to Brisbane Waters) paid the forfeit of their lives on the scaffold in the rear of Sydney Gaol yesterday. The malefactors were all transported felons from the Mother Country, and their names, ages &c were as follows:- Edward Davis, aged 26, arrived in 1833, per ship *Camden*; Robert Chitty, 37, arrived 1829, per *Sophia*; James Everett, 25, arrived 1832 per *Mangles*; John Marshall, 27, arrived in 1832 per *Clyde*; Richard Glanville, 31, arrived 1831 per *Lord Lynedoch* and John Shea, 27, arrived 1837 per *Calcutta.*

These men terminated a long series of systematic burglaries and wholesale plunder by the more heinous crime of deliberate murder. They attacked on the 21st December last, the station of Mr Dangar, at Scone. On meeting with some opposition from Mr Graham, (Mr Dangar's storekeeper) one of the ruffians followed the unfortunate young man into the bush, and deliberately shot him. The notoriety, which the crimes of these men have attained, drew together a large concourse of spectators to witness their execution. The entrance to the Gaol, in George Street, was besieged for admission long before the arrival, at nine o'clock of a strong military guard from the barracks. So great was the pressure of the crowd that it required the unremitting exertions of Captain Innes to preserve order. At ten minutes past nine, the culprits were strongly pinioned and conducted from the cells to the area in front of the drop, where they knelt down. Chitty, Everett, Marshall and Glanville were attended by the Rev. William Cowper and Rev. John Elder. The Rev. Mr Murphy, Catholic Priest accompanied Shea and Mr Isaac Minister of the Jewish congregation in New South Wales, attended Davis (being of the Jewish persuasion). All the culprits (if we except Everett) deeply lamented their having committed the crimes for which they were about to die, and acknowledged the justice of their sentences. Everett ascended the scaffold hurriedly and in an evident state of excitement. He was followed by Chitty, Marshall and Glanville, all three of whom, on reaching the scaffold sung the first verse of the Morning Hymn, as is found in many editions of the book of Common Prayer, commencing, "Awake my soul, and with the sun." This act of devotion we have since heard was entirely spontaneous and not having been suggested, or even expected by either of the reverend gentlemen who attended to administer the consolations of religion according to the rites of the Protestant Church. The ropes were speedily adjusted, and the white caps drawn over the faces of the wretched criminals. In the short interval, which elapsed before the withdrawal of the fatal bolt, Marshall and Glanville were engaged in loud and apparently fervent prayer, and we observed the culprit Davis (who was attired in a suit of mourning), thank the Jewish Minister for the attention paid to him in his last moments. The struggles of all the men were of short duration; the immense crowd dispersed peacefully. It will be remembered that these men were apprehended chiefly through the active exertions of Mr Day, Police Magistrate, of Maitland.

The Australian, Thursday, 18th March 1841

On Tuesday morning last, the six men who have been under sentence of death for the past fortnight, underwent that dread penalty in the Sydney Gaol.
Long before the hour named for bringing the culprits from their cells to be placed on the last stage which they were destined to tread, the gallows yard, it was thronged with persons who had availed themselves of their acquaintance with the gaoler to obtain admittance. At half past eight o'clock, about the gaol doors were congregated a dense group of persons, who edged in abreast, and defined a passage or approach to the gaol doors. It is deservedly worthy of notice, that among the crowd were three persons who were anxious to obtain admittance in their vocation as Reporters to the Public Press, and upon a card being passed from one to another. By this semi-telegraphic mode of conveyance through the little iron grated window, the gate was presently opened, and edged in by some old rusty cutlasses, the Reporters obtained admittance. At nine o'clock, a Captain's guard was drawn up. The yard was emptied of its prison inhabitants, and the two sides being roped off, presented a wide and ample

theatre in which the last sad solemnities of a scene were to be enacted, to which a concourse of some thousand spectators from without and within had been collected.
The neighbouring Church Bell tolled, which was the signal for the departure from their cells of the several culprits. The Rev. Mr Cowper appeared leading, or rather conducting, Marshall Everett, Chitty and Glanville (Glanby); they appeared most fervent in their devotions. Shea was accompanied by Rev. Mr Murphy, and Davis who was of the Hebrew persuasion, was attended by Mr Isaac, the reader to the Synagogue. The latter was attired in a suit of black. The other culprits appeared in the usual prison dress assumed on public executions.

Decidedly this was a most pitiable and melancholy exhibition of its kind. They were all young men. On their trial there was a degree of recklessness and hardihood manifested; not so now – if, for five of these unhappy men it may be judged from the fervour of their devotions, greater manifestations of penitence were never displayed, nor could any Christian minister record of the awful obligation enjoined on him, to cultivate repentance, a death scene more contrite. Davis in truth, it must be said, appeared with a mind unsettled; the enquiring eye turning in glances round the yard, and then upon the group of some hundreds of spectators assembled on the hill above, seemingly in search and recognition of some known friend or acquaintance. In health, strength and energies to all which the buoyancy of almost youth, scarcely arrived at the prime of manhood, these six unhappy men saw placed before them their coffins, and suspended from the beam of the scaffold, the ropes.

The Deputy Sheriff read the warrant assigning one and each for execution, and the clergymen being warned that further time could not be stayed, the culprits rose and one by one mounted that platform. They were in witness of a thousand sights; their sense of existence would have to be terminated by a disgraceful end. Davis remained last. The first four named, spontaneously on ascending the scaffold, commenced singing the morning hymn, used in all protestant and dissenting places of public worship.

How marked the contrast this, to the levity they displayed on their trial, when even the assumption of the black cap, awful prelude to a frightful tragedy, failed to make an impression. The clergymen having remained with the wretched men, as long as the terms of the warrant would allow, the executioner proceeded to his office of placing the caps over their faces and thereby closing upon them forever the light of this world, and all that pertained to it. At this dreadful juncture, the clergymen attendant, two of whom were observed with tears trickling down their aged cheeks, took an affectionate farewell.
The signal being given by the Sub-Sheriff, the bolt was on a sudden withdrawn, and these six misguided young men were launched into eternity. The bodies having hanged the usual time were consigned to the respective coffins.

Australasian Chronicle Thursday, 18th March 1841

On Tuesday morning, the six bushrangers, James Everett, Robert Chitty, John Marshall, Richard Glanville, John Shea and Edward Davis who were convicted at the last criminal sittings of the wilful murder of John Graham at Scone, on the 21st December last, all paid the forfeit of their lives by expiating their offences on the scaffold. An immense crowd was to witness the last awful scene of these men's career, as they had been long notorious for the many burglaries, which they committed in various parts of the interior, but chiefly in the Hunter River district. At a few minutes past nine o'clock the wretched men were conducted from their cells to the area in front of the drop, where they knelt for some time in the exercise of their devotions.

Chitty, Everett, Marshall and Glanville, were attended by Rev. Mr Cowper and the Rev. John Elder; Shea by, the Very Rev. Mr Murphy and Davis, being of the Jewish faith, was attended by Mr Isaac, the Jewish Rabbi. They all appeared to be deeply impressed with a full sense of their awful situation, and paid great attention to the instruction and prayers of their spiritual attendants. After ten minutes spent in devotion they rose, and Everett, in a very hurried manner ran up the steps leading to the scaffold, and was followed by Chitty, Glanville and Marshall; there all four in a loud and clear voice sang the first verse of the hymn commencing –

"Awake my soul, and with the sun"

Shea was the next to ascend, and Davis who was dressed in a suit of mourning, was the last to ascend, he cast his eye with a keen, penetrating glances upon the crowd assembled in the gaol yard as if to recognise any acquaintances, then with a firm step mounted the ladder. A few minutes more were spent in devotion, and then the ropes were adjusted and the cape drawn over their faces; they still continued (particularly Everett and Glanville in loud and apparently fervent prayer till the bolt was drawn and they were launched into the presence of their Maker. They all died almost without a struggle. They had long been a terror to the inhabitants in the district of the Hunter, and it is hoped that the awful example, which has been made of them, will deter others from the pursuing of such lawless practices.

"Awake, my soul, and with the sun
Thy daily stage of duty run;
Shake off dull sloth, and joyful rise,
To pay thy morning sacrifice".[10]

It may be of interest to readers that the St Aubins Inn, licensed in 1840 to George and Elizabeth Chivers still stands and is utilised as a private home.

Guilty or not.

In this case with the various witnesses providing strong evidence, I would have to agree with the jury. The gang appeared to have not one shred of grief for the deceased and acted with malice.

THE AFTERMATH: JOHN ANDERSON ROBERTSON

The lack of activity from Mr John Anderson Robertson, Police Magistrate of Scone, following the attack on Chivers' and Dangar's establishments and the murder of John Graham caused a number of letters and articles to appear in the newspapers of the day. *The Sydney Herald* ran the following letter:-

To the Editor of *The Sydney Herald*, 16 January 1841.
Mr Editor: I have just read an article in the *Sydney Gazette* of yesterday, in defence of Police Magistrates generally, but particularly Mr Robertson, the incumbent of Scone. About the time that article was written by his friend and namesake, Mr Robertson himself communicated to the Governor, he 'had received private information that five or seven bushrangers had robbed a sheep station at Muswellbrook, belonging to Sir Francis Forbes and he intended to proceed in pursuit of them tomorrow, but neither on this, or the former occasion had he received any information from the Police at Muswellbrook.'
Now Mr Editor, this censure implied on Mr Allman, a brave, active and intelligent magistrate, ought not to pass unnoticed. I will therefore contrast the services of these two paid magistrates and let the public judge of their efficiency.
About ten days ago, Mr Allman received information that Sir Francis Forbes' station near Muswellbrook had been robbed; he immediately assembled a force and pursued the robbers, and in two or three hours, after the robbery had been committed the offenders were in his custody with all the plunder. Had he waited till tomorrow, as Mr Robertson did, many other depredations might have been committed by the same party before they were secured. Mr Robertson is easily imposed on; and in all probability, the 'private information' he has received alludes to the same robbery, and tomorrow he is going to pursue the persons who have been safely lodged in gaol the last ten days. What Mr R. means by 'the previous occasion' I do not comprehend. I will however show you what his conduct was at Scone on the 21st December when the bushrangers robbed Mr William Dangar's house, Mr Thomas Dangar's store, Chivers the innkeeper and shot Mr Graham. These all occurred early in the morning close to the residence of the Police Magistrate. When Mr Day and his party arrived about three hours after these outrages he was found writing very composedly fifty yards from the spot where the dead body was lying and had made no arrangements for the capture of the murderers, nor did he accompany Mr Day in the pursuit, nor even send one of his constables. The murderers were secured by Mr Day's party the same evening at a distance of 70 miles and brought back to Scone, but not committed for trial by Mr Robertson. They were remanded from that bench to Muswellbrook and there committed. This, I believe, was reported to government, yet, to the surprise of the whole colony, Mr Robertson is still in office[15]. [Anonymous]

The letter referred to by the anonymous person writing to the *Sydney Herald* was as follows:

The Hon. The Colonial Secretary, Sydney

Police office, Scone 8 January 1841

Sir,
Information having this morning reached me that five or eight armed Bushrangers had attacked a station of Judge Forbes's near Muswellbrook and that the Town of Muswellbrook had been under arms all night, and as it was believed that a second attack would be made on the Township, I lost not a moment in putting this place in a state of defence, and in calling in the Ticket of Leave men of this District with horses and rations, and shall tomorrow proceed with mounted party of these men in search of the Bushrangers.

---

[10] http://cyberhymnal.org/htm/a/w/awakemys.htm

> The information relative to the Bushrangers reached this place by private hand, and I have reason to complain that both on the present occasion, and the late one, no information has ever been sent on by the Police at Muswellbrook tho on both occasions the Police there have had a day's notice of previous information.
> I have the honour to be,
> Sir,
> Your most obt Servt, J A Robertson JP.

The letter was received in Sydney on 13th January 1841 and provoked the following response from George Gipps, Governor:

> Acknowledge receipt – I say that though I approve of his calling in the Ticket of Leave Holders, I do not understand why he deferred his pursuit of the Bushrangers till the next day.
> Write to Mr Allman and request to know what measures he has taken in consequence of the appearance of these men. GG.

Francis Allman Jnr, Police Magistrate Muswellbrook responded that the report Mr Robertson received re bushrangers at Muswellbrook was without foundation and that the Muswellbrook district was 'perfectly quiet.'[16]

Mr Robertson was a prolific letter writing and he retained his position. Perhaps the fact that his brother was a Lord may have assisted him.[17]

Francis Allman (above),
Governor George Gipps (right).

CASE 7 - 1843 **MERTON [DENMAN]**

JOHN RUTLEDGE **DECEASED VICTIM**

BENJAMIN HARRIS **ACCUSED MURDERER**

PERSONS FOR THE PROSECUTION

Robert Leaton	**convict**
Patrick Dawe	**hutkeeper at Captain Pike's station**
William Everness	**Chief Constable at Merton**
Patrick Doyle	**constable at Cassilis, TL holder**

PERSONS FOR THE DEFENCE

No legal person for his defence

Robert Eden	**knew prisoner**
Charles Boydell	**Juror, knew prisoner**

John Rutledge is a typical example of those who pass through an area leaving very little information regarding themselves. In this case we know that he was a police constable stationed at Cassilis. He was married and had three children.

TWENTY-FIVE POUNDS REWARD, OR A FREE PARDON.
Maitland Mercury 20th May 1843

The bushranger who shot Constable Rutledge about twelve miles from Merton, on the 6th instant, an account of which we gave in our last[11], has not yet been apprehended. It appears the murder was witnessed by the two other prisoners whom Rutledge had in custody, as well as the hut keeper of the place where it occurred, none of whom attempted to stop the murderer when he escaped. The unfortunate constable left a wife and three children to deplore his untimely fate. The name of the murderer is Benjamin Harris per ship "James Laing", a runaway from the Newcastle boat's crew. The government has offered a reward of £25 to any free person who may apprehend and lodge him in any of her Majesty's gaols; and if he is apprehended by a prisoner of the Crown, application will be made to her Majesty for a free pardon.

Description: Benjamin Harris, per ship *James Laing*, a runaway from the Newcastle Boat's Crew, 37 years of age, born Staffordshire, a soldier, 5' 5¾" in height, sallow complexion, brown hair, hazel grey eyes, JHEHL knot, wreath, BH inside lower right arm, sun inside lower left arm, heart and 7 dots back of left hand.

CAPTURE OF HARRIS
Maitland Mercury Saturday, 8th July 1843
Harris the bushranger who murdered Constable Rutledge of Cassilis, while under escort in May last en route to Merton, was captured on the 28th ult. by Constable Doyle, of the Cassilis establishment. The prisoner is now on his route to Merton in which district he stands charged with the murder of Rutledge. Doyle is a prisoner of the Crown holding the Governor's ticket, and it is hoped that his Excellency will for the praiseworthy conduct he has displayed on this occasion grant him a free pardon. He has been out a month, fully determined to apprehend Harris, and he captured him without assistance.

THE WIDOW OF CONSTABLE RUTLEDGE
Maitland Mercury 15th July 1843

We are happy to hear that £50 has been raised by subscription in this neighbourhood, and a similar sum has been given by the government, for the use and support of the wife and family of the late Constable Rutledge who was shot by Harris the bushranger.

[11] This report has not been located.

Maitland Circuit Court
SMH Saturday 25th September 1843
Benjamin Harris was indicted for the wilful murder of John Rutledge by shooting him with a gun, on the 5th May last, at Merton.

The following persons gave evidence:

Robert Leaton – was a prisoner of the Crown and in April last he was punished by the Merton Bench and ordered to be returned to the Government. He was given in charge to Constable Rutledge, along with the prisoner at the bar and another man to be brought to Merton. Leaton stated the constable had a musket and ammunition belt and pouch. They arrived at Pickering about ten o'clock on the morning of the third day and they went into the hut. In a few minutes Rutledge came in leaving his musket outside. The prisoner went out, took the musket and presented it to the constable, stating if he did not give up his ammunition, he would put its contents through him. The constable refused to give it and went out. Harris stepped back a step or two and fired the musket. Witness went out directly after and saw Rutledge lying on the ground dead. The ammunition belt was taken from his body; the ball entered just below the stomach. The prisoner made off when witness went out of the hut and he saw no more of him until he was apprehended. Witness and the other prisoner went back and gave themselves up.

Patrick Dawe, hutkeeper at Captain Pike's station: Remembered a constable and two or three prisoners coming to the station; he did not know the constable, the prisoners were in charge [of Constable Rutledge], one of them had a pair of handcuffs on; the last witness was one of those in charge; he could not say whether the prisoner was. The prisoners went into the hut and sat down, the constable came in and went to the fire. The prisoner next the door went out, took up the musket, cocked it and demanded the ammunition from the constable. The prisoners were not chained or linked together. The constable approached him and said 'Do it!' Prisoner said he would if he did not give up his ammunition, prisoner drew back and the constable went out and witness soon after heard the report of the musket. Witness went out, saw the constable lying on the ground and the prisoner took away the ammunition belt and pouch and went away with the musket. The other prisoners said they would give themselves up and left the hut for that purpose.

William Everness, chief constable at Merton: Knew Constable Rutledge, his name was John. Witness went to Captain Pike's station in May last and saw Rutledge dead, the body was covered with a piece of bark about fifteen or twenty yards from the hut. There was a gun-shot wound in the belly, witness found three warrants in his coat pocket. He had known Rutledge about five or six years and had known the prisoner about the same time. The prisoner had been a watchman on Mr Blaxland's station.

Patrick Doyle: Knew the prisoner, apprehended him on 25th last as a bushranger. The magistrates ordered him to be forwarded to Newcastle to be dealt with. Witness saw him off with escort and on 8th May, heard of the murder and set out in pursuit on the 14th and apprehended him on the 27th June still with the constable's ammunition, pouch and musket on him. He delivered him up to the Merton Bench, the belt and musket were produced in Court and identified.

This closed the case for the Crown.

The prisoner put in a written defence which was read, and in which he stated that the constable was shot by him accidentally.

Robert Eden: Had known the prisoner for some years, did not know that he had anything amiss in his mind; had never observed that he was easily excited by drink.

Charles Boydell, one of the jurors: knew the prisoner as a shepherd in the late John Blaxland's employment, he was much given to drinking and Mr Blaxland said when in liquor he appeared to lose his senses, which Mr Blaxland attributed to some wounds which he had received in his head while a soldier.

His Honor then summed up and the Jury without retiring from the box, returned a verdict of guilty. His Honor then passed sentence of death upon the prisoner in a solemn and impressive manner, exhorting him to prepare for eternity, as there could be no hope of mercy shown towards him in this world.

ORDER FOR EXECUTION
Maitland Mercury 14th October 1843
Benjamin Harris for murder of Constable Rutledge ordered for execution at Newcastle on 17th instant.

EXECUTION

Maitland Mercury 21st October 1843

The execution of the unfortunate man, Benjamin Harris took place on Tuesday last, about nine o'clock in the forenoon. He was attended on the awful occasion by several gentlemen of the Wesleyan Methodist connection. He met his fate with great fortitude, and died without a struggle.

Some points to consider:

- It is approximately 60 miles from Cassilis to Merton, three prisoners with only one person in charge and only one with handcuffs who was not the accused.
- There is no mention of horses so it is assumed the prisoners and guard were on foot.
- Harris may have had a medical problem that would be assessed more carefully in today's climate.
- A juror spoke in Harris's defence?

No records have been located that records the burial place of Rutledge. Was he buried at Merton, Pickering or taken back to Cassilis.

Some background on John Rutledge. He arrived in NSW in 1833 per *Asia* as a convict under a sentence of transportation for life. He was 29 years of age, could read and write, Protestant and was a married man. He was a native of Lancashire and a blacksmith (indifferent) and a soldier. He was tried at a Gibraltar Court Martial for desertion. He had one previous sentence of three months gaol.

John was 5' 9" in height, dark sallow complexion, brown hair and hazel eyes. Distinguishing feature were a thick nose, scar on back of left hand, scar on 4th finger of left hand and a D [deserter] tattooed under left arm.
In 1837 he was located at Cassilis working for Alexander Bushby as an assigned servant. On 11 May 1840 his sentence of life was reduced to 14 years. It is unknown when he joined the Cassilis Police as a constable[18].

The reader may be wondering what happened to Mrs Rutledge. Some information has been located that indicates she was the post mistress at Cassilis between 1836 and 1839[19]. This may not be correct. On 1st May 1845 application was made by Robert Everard to marry Mary Ann Rutledge. He was a convict holding a T of L[12] and required the government's permission to marry. The application stated he was 35 years of age, arrived per *Planter* under a sentence of life, but by 1845 held the indulges of a T of L. Mary Jane aged 30 arrived in NSW per *Canton* and came free. The *Canton* arrived September 1841 carrying emigrants and passengers, but only the cabin passengers and emigrants were named. Mary Ann most likely arrived under a scheme which allowed convicts to bring their families to NSW. The marriage of Robert and Mary Ann in 1845 appears in the records of St Phillips C of E, Sydney. The following year they had a son who was named Robert[20].

In January 1849 Robert Everard was granted a conditional pardon which meant he was a free man on condition he remain within the colony, but in July he suddenly became ill and died. The inquest found he 'died by the visitation of God'[21].

Back on 1 November 1843 Mary Ann had purchased Allotment 7 in the village of Dalkeith, but the land was not formerly conveyed until 21 January 1848 due to the death of Robert Scott, the previous owner[22].

There are many gaps in the information concerning Mary Ann. At the beginning of this account the *Maitland Mercury* informed us that the death of John Rutledge left her a widow with three children. An attempt was made to locate the marriage to John Rutledge and the birth of the children without success. In 1854 Mary Ann made a will which provides the name of one child.

> Will of Mary Anne Everett [later corrected to Everard] of Dalkeith, district of Cassilis, widow, I leave all real and personal property to my son William Rutledge and appoint him sole executor of my estate. 4 February 1854[23]

It is unknown when Mary Ann died, but on 3 September 1863 William Wilson Rutledge of Cassilis, stock keeper transferred Lot 7, Dalkeith to Edward Scully of Cassilis, constable for £25. Note stated Mary Ann Everard, late of Cassilis, widow, formerly Mary Ann Rutledge was the mother of William Wilson Rutledge[24]. No mention of any other children.

---

[12] T of L, ticket of leave which allowed a convict to work on their own account in a designated district.

CASE 8 - 1846 **JERRY'S PLAINS**

VICTIM **NAME UNKNOWN**

MURDERER **NAME UNKNOWN**

BODY FOUND AT REDBANK, JERRY'S PLAINS
Maitland Mercury Saturday, 6 June 1846

On Tuesday evening a stepson of Mr Harper's, the postmaster, who had been in the bush looking for cattle, brought home a quantity of human bones, which he had discovered in a gully about three or four miles from Jerry's Plains. As they were evidently the remains of a human being, and the youth stated there were more of a similar kind, half reduced to ashes amongst the embers of a fire that had been made in the same place, together with burnt portions of clothing (a specimen of which he had also brought with him), Mr Harper gave notice to the sergeant of the Mounted Police, and this morning, in company with that gentleman, Mr Donnelly, and the boy, started to make an examination of the place described.

Between three and four miles from Jerry's Plains, in a gully leading from Redbank Creek, and within a short distance of Mr Hale's fence, they at length succeeded in finding the place, where, from what presented itself to their inspection, there can be no doubt the awful crime of murder had been consummated only a few weeks previously.

The fire had been made in the bottom of a water-course that ran through the gully, between two shelving banks of red earth, and the wood for it had apparently been collected here and there on either side of the gully. On the surface of the coals and ashes, for some of the wood remained, there were the arm bones, ribs etc of a human being; portions of the clothing also, adhering to the flesh, which had been reduced by the fire to a black, porous, shining sort of substance, were plentifully scattered through the whole.

Supposing, from the difficulty of consuming the head, that it might have been secreted elsewhere, a search was made at the end of the fire where, from the position of the body it should have lain, and portions of the skull, jawbones, and some of the teeth, were raked out. At the opposite end of the heap were found the charred heels of a pair of strong boots, the shoemaker's sprigs still sticking in them in regular rows. On the top of the bank, immediately above the fire, were the signs of a considerable quantity of blood, as if the body had been laid there for some time previously to being rolled down, or probably, as was supposed, the murder had been committed.
About a couple of yards from the spot the sergeant picked up the haft of a knife, resembling the haft of a shoemaker's knife, but composed of colonial wood; and, after making some remarks about it, suggested that the blade might be found in the ashes.

A fresh search was accordingly made, and just about the middle of the fire a sharp-pointed blade, about seven inches long, was pointed out, a quantity of burnt blood still adhering to it, and which fitted exactly to the handle previously found.

Maitland Mercury Wednesday 10th June 1846

On Friday last Captain Russel JP and Dr Vallack arrived from Singleton to hold an inquest upon the remains of the human skeleton that had been discovered near the Redbank Creek.

After inspecting the portion of the remains that had been brought to the post office, consisting of the sacrum, lumbar, a part of the dorsal vertebrae with some of the ribs attached, the upper part of the thighbone and hip (os femoris and pelvis), still connected in their sockets by their natural ligaments, which appeared quite unctuous and fresh. Captain Russell took the depositions of the persons who had discovered them. Then, accompanied by the Doctor, Mr Harpur and Sergeant Edwards, proceeded to Redbank, for the purpose of making a personal and more particular examination of the spot in which the body had been consumed.

On reaching the place of the murder, the Captain remarked, in reference to the wild and desolate character of the surrounding country, "that it was indeed a fitting place for the perpetration of a deed of darkness."

The fire had evidently been made and carefully tended by the murderer with the view of consuming the body of his victim. Not a particle of the wood remained unburned, and even the coals appeared to have been so kept together as to be mostly reduced to ashes. But thickly mixed through the ashes, and even preponderating in quality, were the bones, most of them entirely calcined, yet retaining their form, and a few quite fresh, as of but recently stripped of their integuments, together with lumps of charred flesh and burnt fragments of clothing.

After inspecting the place and the marks of blood at a few yards distance there from, Captain Russell fully concurred in the opinion that a murder had been committed, and an attempt there made to make away with the remains of the murdered individual. The Doctor was of the opinion that it might have taken place within the last two months or less. The fragments of clothing found unconsumed in the ashes consist of a small piece of a blue-stripped flannel frock or shirt (the stripes of which, when worn, it is supposed, would be in a sideways or lateral direction), and of a somewhat larger portion of a Guernsey frock, stripped with chains of blue triangular spots, which stripes, it is supposed, in the wearing would take an up and down or perpendicular direction. The latter frock is likely to have been worn over the former. It is the sort of clothing generally worn by bullock-drivers and their mates, amongst which class of persons this horrible transaction is supposed to have taken place.

It is to be hoped that all persons, and particularly those in the habit of travelling with teams, will communicate any suspicious circumstances that may happen to fall within their knowledge to the police, it being an acknowledged rule in all grades of society to render every assistance towards the detection of the murderer.

No report has been found that indicates who the murdered person was or that the murderer had been apprehended.

Some thoughts:

- It appears that no crime scene was established.
- A search was not made for tracks of a dray or some other sort of vehicle.
- No reward was offered by the government for information.
- Strange that the handle of the broken knife was left at the scene or not tossed in the fire. Was the murderer disturbed and left the scene?
- What happen to the bones of the victim?

Perhaps this was the perfect crime.

Captain Russell, later a Member of the NSW Parliament.

CASE 9 - 1846 **CASSILIS**

TOMMY **DECEASED VICTIM**

UNKNOWN **ACCUSED MURDERER**

Maitland Mercury Wednesday 10th June 1846[13]

The discovery was made of the murder of an Aboriginal native named Tommy by his sable brethren. The body was discovered on Saturday last by the chief constable of Cassilis, accompanied by the overseer of a sheep station called Derigery and a black gin who lived with Tommy, and who is supposed to have been the cause of the murder. It was concealed in one of the ridges near Reedy Creek about four miles from the above station. The blacks have not been seen about since the murder was reported, although great pains have been taken to search them out, as the magistrates are determined to get to the bottom the affair, in consequence of a suspicion that the blacks have been instigated by a white man with whom the same gin formerly lived, and who is said to have offered a reward to the blacks to bring her back to him.

Tommy was a superior specimen of his race, having been taught habits of industry by some person now living in Parramatta. He was latterly employed on the sheep station above named, and would demand a settlement with his employer the same as a white man. The murder is supposed to have been committed on the 24th May; it was reported to the overseer on the 29th; and on Saturday last the overseer reported it to the police.

Some thoughts:

- There is a long delay between when it is believed the murder took place and being reported to the police.
- Who was the white man that Tommy's partner had lived with?
- Was she questioned?

Aboriginal campfire, with squatter, by S.T. Gill 1840s.

[13] While some of the words in this newspaper account may be offensive to some persons it is the language of that period.

CASE 10 - 1847 **CASSILIS**

JOSEPH PALFREY **DECEASED VICTIM**

JOHN PURCELL **ACCUSED MURDERER**

PERSONS FOR THE PROSECUTION

Barbarra McDonald	**settler, living about five miles from deceased and accused**
John Grice	**Sergeant in Mounted Police, based at Cassilis**
James Brady	**superintendent for Mr Tindal, took up station of Palfrey and Purcell**
Adolphus Jones	**settler, son of late John Jones, Turee**
Thomas Clarke	**overseer for Mr Blackstone**
Thomas Kerr	**Chief Constable, Cassilis**
Alfred John Nichol	**surgeon, Cassilis**
Michael McCartney	**surgeon, Maitland**

PERSONS FOR THE DEFENCE

Mr Purefoy	**solicitor**

This is a long and complicated case involving two partners who took up a grazing lease between Merriwa and Cassilis in the 1840s. One of the partners was married with a young family.

The main characters are John Purcell, Roman Catholic married to Bridget, they had at least two children. The other was Joseph Palfrey, a half-brother of John Ryder Jones and Adolphus Bartlett Jones.

If you refer back to Case No. 3 you will find that Joseph Palfrey was the step-son of John Jones who was murdered in 1837.

Again, this case relies on the newspaper reports for information.

CASSILIS: SUSPECTED MURDER

Maitland Mercury 9th June 1847

I informed you in my last that the chief constable of this place [Cassilis] had gone to the Goulburn to assist in the search for Mr Joseph Palfrey who had been missed under suspicious circumstances[14].

Mr Palfrey had resided at the junction of the Lett[15] and Goulburn Rivers, and was in partnership with a person named John Purcell. About the middle of May he disappeared suddenly, and strong suspicions were entertained that he had been murdered. A strict search was commenced by several of his friends, headed by two of his half-brothers, the Messrs Jones but to no purpose, and suspicions being strongly excited against Purcell, notice was sent to the Cassilis police. Chief Constable Kerr and the sergeant of the mounted police immediately proceeded to the spot, and the search was resumed, but without success. Purcell was however, apprehended, and forwarded to Cassilis.

Among the parties assisting in the search were Mr Blackstone, of Mudgee; Mr Clarke, overseer to Mr. B and Mr Brady overseer to another gentleman.

After all search was given up as fruitless, Mr Brady, with one of his men, went to the river Lett to form a sheep station, and in doing so chancing to pass about a hundred yards from Mr Palfrey's late residence, he observed his dog scraping away the sand from a particular spot very diligently. Stopping to watch the dog, Mr B observed some flies about the place; he drew the ramrod from his gun, and thrust it into the earth, which he found to be loose, but that something hard was beneath. On drawing up the rod, he saw as it were, two threads adhering to the top of it, and noticed that the flies began to pass down the hole which the rod had made. A spade was sent for, and after digging a hole to the depth of about eighteen inches, Mr Brady and his assistant came to what they thought was the stump or root of a tree, and were about to abandon their labour, when they fortunately struck on the end of the log. On removing it they found a bag, which, on examination, was found to contain the body of Mr Palfrey.

---

[14] Unable to locate this report on Trove.

[15] Unable to locate the Lett River though local residents believe it may have been an early name for the Krui River.

The place where the body was found is on the bank of the Lett, and about a hundred yards from the house. The body was covered again with care, and a guard being set on the place, intelligence was sent to Cassilis from whence the authorities are going to hold an investigation.

THE MURDER ON THE GOULBURN

Maitland Mercury 23rd June 1847

I have before informed you of the discovery of the body of the late Mr Joseph Palfrey, and of the apprehension of his partner, John Purcell on suspicion of murdering him. On Wednesday last Purcell was committed for trial on the charge of wilful murder, by the bench. On Friday he was forwarded from this place [Cassilis], on his way to Newcastle Gaol, under the charge of Chief Constable Kerr, and the sergeant of the mounted police. June 20th, 1847.

THE MURDER ON THE GOULBURN

Maitland Mercury Saturday 26th June 1847

Cassilis 19th June 1847: John Purcell in custody here on suspicion of having murdered Joseph Palfrey whose body had been found buried on the bank of the river Lett, near its junction with the Goulburn, as reported in the *Mercury* on the 9th instant, was on Wednesday last committed by the Cassilis bench to take his trial for the murder.

The evidence adduced is entirely of a circumstantial nature, partly derived from the expression of the prisoner after he had been informed that suspicion rested entirely on him. The ostensible reason alleged for the perpetration of the horrible deed is, that better than three years ago, Palfrey (the deceased) had formed a criminal intimacy with Bridget Purcell the prisoner's wife, which continued up to the time of this fatal occurrence.

[The term 'criminal intimacy' is an archaic term more akin to adultery which in itself was not a criminal offence. The husband could sue the man committing adultery with his wife seeking damages. This action highlighted the perceived property aspect of a wife in the Victorian era.]

From the evidence of Barbara McDonald taken at the inquest on the 8th instant, at the Goulburn, where the body was found, and which evidence was read to the prisoner, he not being present at the inquest, and Mrs McDonald not being able to attend the court from illness, it was shewn that on the 10th of May last, Palfrey and Purcell's wife came to witness's hut, distant about five miles from the residence of Palfrey. Mrs Purcell was left there by Palfrey, who was going from home, and said he would be back on the following Saturday, when he would take Mrs Purcell away.

This is the last account given of Palfrey, until his body was found. This witness further stated that Mrs Purcell hearing of Palfrey's being missing, left and went home to see if the story were true. She left her children with witness, and sometime after, about the 20th May, Purcell (the prisoner) came to see one of the children, which were left by Mrs Purcell. Witness asked him if Palfrey had returned. Prisoner replied, "Palfrey did not go to come back," and began to cry. He said, "My wife told me that she never would take a day with me while Palfrey lived. Palfrey thought he had a long head, but my head was too long for him."

[The statement, 'Palfrey thought he had a long head, but my head was too long for him' is an interesting observation by Purcell. Purcell is not commenting on the shape or size of their heads but is a metaphorical statement that Palfrey thought he was being clever, but Purcell believed he was the smarter of the two.]

Mr James Brady, superintendent to William Tindal at Bylong, deposed that he had some business with the deceased, and on the 10th May he went to his residence, he saw the prisoner John Purcell at Palfrey's doing something to a green hide rope and asked him if Palfrey was at home; prisoner replied in the negative, and turned into the hut. On witness going away he asked prisoner when it was likely Palfrey would return; he said he could not exactly say, as Palfrey went away sometimes and stayed nine or ten days without saying when he would return. Witness met prisoner again on Mr Tindal's run at Crabby Creek in the course of four or five days after, when he asked him if Palfrey had returned yet; he said, "No indeed, he has not." Prisoner told witness that the horse "Taffy" which Palfrey had been riding, came home without a bridle, and only one stirrup to the saddle; that the horse appeared to have been very much ridden; so much so that he would not feed with the other horses. Witness observed that something must have happened to Palfrey. Prisoner said, "It looks like it." Witness and prisoner, after leaving a hut belonging to John Heany rode together for two miles. Witness said something must have happened Palfrey, and if he were not found prisoner would certainly be taken by police. Prisoner answered, "Now what will you advise me to do in the case?" Witness said report it to the Joneses. On the 26th, witness and Heany went to the late residence of Palfrey to search for the body on and about the River Goulburn, where witness met A Jones and others. Witness said to them, "Tomorrow we will start early, and search for the body all round this place." Prisoner, on hearing this resolution expressed by witness, called him aside and said, 'I see everything is going against me. I find my wife is going against me, for she asked me where a certain tomahawk was, as if she wanted to make people believe that I killed him with the tomahawk.' Prisoner pointed to an old black stump between hut and where the body was afterwards found, and said he got the tomahawk there, and gave it to her; that Palfrey had used it there in the cutting of a limb from a tree. Prisoner wished witness to make out a piece of writing, conveying his property to the children. Witness did so; and while making out the deed or will, prisoner said he would like it was done, as the police would be there soon and take him. Witness observed that the way in which prisoner's wife and Palfrey had been living had made him unhappy. Prisoner replied, 'O yes, I put up with it long enough; but I am satisfied; it will never happen again.' After the prisoner had been taken into custody, witness continued his search for the body, which he at last found, on the 5th instant, after an unremitting search; for which the witness received the thanks of the bench.

The evidence of John Heany went to show that Mrs Purcell, prisoner's wife, came to the hut; she found Palfrey's stock whip and a spur which he had borrowed for the journey, as well as some articles of clothing' and observed that if Palfrey had gone from home he would have taken them.

The evidence of Thomas Clark, overseer to Mr Blackstone of Drummer's Flat, proved that the horse, 'Taffy' was not distressed by hard riding, as was stated by the prisoner, and that he (Clark) suggested to Mrs Purcell to ask her husband where a tomahawk was which was then missing from among the tools belonging to the hut; and in the interim he said to prisoner, 'Purcell you must have made away with Palfrey' Prisoner exclaimed, 'The Lord have mercy on me, I can die but once.' Mrs Purcell asked prisoner for the tomahawk. Prisoner asked her what she wanted it for, and on her answering that she had laid it covering something in an old pair of shoes, and that she found it was removed, prisoner said, 'I understand now why you are asking for the tomahawk.' Clark examined the tomahawk afterwards, which was put into his hands by Mrs Purcell, but could discern no stains. (Here the tomahawk was put into the hands of the witness, but he stated that his sight was not perfect.)

The Chief Constable stated that he, accompanied by Sergeant Grice went with the warrant to apprehend prisoner. They told him what they came for. Prisoner was not at all startled, but, on the contrary, quite composed. The tomahawk was pointed out to witness, lying at the end of the hut. He examined it, and found that, although it had been acted on by the rain, which had about the time fallen, there was still some coagulated substance thereon, and he had every reason to believe it was blood. He found also adhering to the back of the tomahawk one human hair, of the colour of that of Palfrey's when alive.

Dr Nicol attended the inquest on the 8th instant, when the body was identified. A hole, three feet wide and four feet long, was pointed out to him in the bed of the river, in which the body was lying with its face downwards. On its removal to the bank, the upper part of the body was found to be enclosed in a sack, which contained some grass, with the legs crossed; it had on a striped shirt, cord trousers, and cotton socks. Decomposition had far advanced, particularly about the head and face, so as to make it difficult to discern any external marks of violence, with the exception of a depression on the right side of the head. On examining the skull, he found the right side completely shattered, and several portions of the bone pressing on the brain, and described the fractures to be the result of two blows, at least, with a heavy blunt instrument, such as the tomahawk produced. In the opinion of the witness, from the appearances of the body, life must have been extinct three weeks; and from the saturated appearance of the clothes, he was inclined to think the body had been first thrown into water. Instant death must have succeeded the blows. There was no appearance of any struggle, except the hands being closed inwards, which might have been caused by the action of the nerves. The blows must have been given from behind by some person standing to the left.

The prisoner declined saying anything in his defence. He is a man apparently between thirty and forty years of age.

Reported from Singleton 25th June 1847: John Purcell, charged with the murder of the late Mr Palfrey, arrived at the Singleton lockup on Tuesday last, on his way to Newcastle Gaol. The wretched man seems to be in a very distressed state of mind[25].

Maitland Circuit Court: Murder, Before Mr Justice Therry
Maitland Mercury, Monday, September 13th, 1847.

John Purcell, late of Cassilis was indicted for having, on the 15th May 1847, committed an assault on Joseph Palfrey at the Rivulet, and with some unknown blunt instrument wounded him on the right side of the head, of which wound Palfrey instantly died; and that thus the said John Purcell did feloniously kill and murder the said Joseph Palfrey.

Mr Purefoy appeared for the defence.

The Solicitor General stated the case to the jury, and called:

Barbara McDonald who deposed that she lived about five miles from the prisoner's place, who resided on the Rivulet, and the deceased Palfrey lived with him. On the 10th May Palfrey and Mrs Purcell came to witness's house with two of Mrs P's children. Mrs P. and the children remained for several days, but Palfrey returned home, and called again on the 14th, when he remained a short time, borrowing a spur from witness before he left.

On Tuesday morning, following, prisoner came to see his family just before breakfast. In answer to Mrs Purcell's questions, prisoner said that Palfrey left home on horseback on Saturday afternoon, and was going to Reedy Creek after a horse. Eight days after, on Friday, the 28th May, the prisoner came again, to see his daughter, who had been left there by Mrs Purcell a few days before. Witness asked him if Palfrey had come back, prisoner replied, no, that he did not go for coming back. Prisoner then talked of making his will, and said he wished to leave his cattle and money. Witness asked him why he thought of this, and he replied that his wife was talking about hanging him, and only that there was nobody to look after the two children; she would have been settled too. Prisoner further said that his wife had told him that she would never live with him while Palfrey was alive, but she would not live with Palfrey now; and that Palfrey thought he had a long head, but that his (prisoner's) head was too long for him. Witness cautioned him as to what he would meet after death, as his words implied a determination to destroy himself. Witness never saw Palfrey again alive, but nearly four weeks after he was at her place she saw him lying dead in his hut.

By Mr Purefoy: Witness had lived in these parts six years, and had known these parties four years; witness's memory was good; she would not speak positively unless she was certain.

John Grice deposed that he was a sergeant in the mounted police, and that on the 15th May he went to prisoner's station looking for a strayed horse; witness found the horse, and it being late in the evening he stopped at the hut for the night; there was no one there but the prisoner. In conversation at supper prisoner told him that Palfrey had left home to go to Reedy Creek, to get a horse from his half-brother, John Jones, either that day or the day previous. After supper prisoner said he would change his shirt, but witness observed that he did not put a cleaner one on. Witness had ridden to the hut by the most direct road for Palfrey to have gone to Reedy Creek, but did not meet him.
By Mr Purefoy: Witness stopped at a station called Coggan on the way; half a dozen people might have passed while he was there, but a few passed without calling.

James Brady deposed that in May and June last he was superintendent of Mr Tindal's station at Bylong, about twenty miles from prisoner's station. On Wednesday, the 19th May, witness called at prisoner's and found him alone; witness dined with him, and asked for Palfrey, whom he wanted to see, but prisoner told him that he had gone for a horse that was in the possession of Adolphus Jones his half-brother. When witness left, he asked when he should call again to see Palfrey prisoner said it would be hard for him to say when he would be home, for sometimes he would be away one, two or ten days without their knowing when he would be back.

Witness called again on Saturday, but found no one at home. On the following day prisoner came to witness's nearest out-station, where witness was at the time, and witness told prisoner he had been at his hut, and asked if Palfrey was come home. Prisoner replied "no, indeed, he is not," and added that the previous day he had been out on his run, and found Palfrey horse running with the other horses, having a saddle and one stirrup on, but no bridle, and that the horse looked fatigued.

Witness said something wrong must have happened to Palfrey and went outside to get his horse ready. He then heard prisoner, who had remained inside, tell his hut keeper, John Heeny[16] to go and take this horse and put it on his run, or else, as it was a stray horse. Adolphus Jones, who was coming to his place in a day or two, would be sure to take it away if he found it there, and Palfrey away. Prisoner then came out, and witness and he rode about three miles together. In conversing on the way prisoner admitted that this looked as if something had happened to Palfrey and said that he had not been able to go to look for him yet, as he had been up looking for cattle. Witness advised him to do so at once, and report the occurrence to Messrs Jones, as he being the last man who could give

[16] Also referred to as Heany.

any account of him, he would certainly be called on to account for his disappearance, and he ought also to raise the neighbours to search for him.

Prisoner said he had gone to Mr Jones's, but they did not trouble themselves much about it. Witness said he could not believe that, and that he would return himself as soon as he had done his business, and gather the neighbours, and search for Palfrey Witness did so without success. On the following Wednesday witness went again to Purcell's hut by the river, having picked up Mr Jones at Coggan, and they went to the hut together. They found there three men, named Hewitt, Moore and Clarke. Heeny arrived shortly afterwards. In a short time prisoner, who had been out, came in also and the next day they all searched near the house and further off, but unsuccessfully. Mrs Purcell was then at home. When they returned to the hut in the afternoon witness had a conversation with the prisoner, and drew up for him a pencil copy of a will, by which he left his cattle between his children and his money to his wife. Prisoner remarked that the cattle would never do him any good, but might do some to his children. Witness suggested his appointing Mr Tindal a trustee, and prisoner said he would go to Dabee and ask Mr T.'s permission.

Witness then, in the presence of prisoner, and by his desire, handed over prisoner's money, about £19, to Mrs Purcell. Prisoner next day went over to bring his child from Mrs McDonald's, and witness, who had slept at the hut, went out again on the search. When witness returned in the afternoon, he found prisoner at home, chopping wood, and they entered into conversation. Witness asked him if his child had come home; prisoner replied no; witness asked him why he had given up his money to his wife, when he would want it himself if taken to court, prisoner said he should not be taken to the court, that the police would come, but they would not find him. Witness asked if he meant to run away; prisoner replied no, he should not be far off, but they would not take him to court. Witness then charged him with thinking of destroying himself, which prisoner admitted he did, but by remonstrance, witness induced him to say he would endeavour to alter his mind.

Witness said, "It appears that the way in which your wife lived with Palfrey has made you very unhappy;" prisoner replied, "Yes, I have been very unhappy for many a long day;" witness said, "It does not appear as though Palfrey was coming to annoy you again;" prisoner replied, "No, I am satisfied;" and he added, "I thought there was some hope for me until this woman asked me about the tomahawk." By this woman prisoner meant his wife, and he alluded to something that had occurred during witness's absence. Prisoner said that Clarke had put the woman up to asking him where was the tomahawk – and that at first, he would not give them that satisfaction, but that in a minute or two he fetched it to them. Witness asked where it had been; prisoner replied that it had been sticking in a stump by the bank of the Rivulet, at a short distance from the house, where Palfrey had it last to drive in a nail, and to cut off a small branch. On the Saturday morning, by witness's advice, prisoner started to go to Mr Tindal's, and witness accompanied him part way, it being about fifty miles off. Witness again saw prisoner at his hut on the Monday evening following in the hands of the police, but little conversation passed between them. Prisoner was then removed to Cassilis in custody, and after all search was given up, witness, who knew Mrs Purcell meant to leave the spot, went to the neighbourhood of the hut again to establish a sheep station.

He went there about two hours in advance of Heeny, who was to follow him. Witness went to water his horse at a deep waterhole in the bed of the Rivulet, in front of the hut, and about a hundred yards from it, and in returning from the waterhole he saw, at a few yards distance, a small space scratched by a dog's paw, and noticed three large flies settled on it. Witness disturbed the flies, but they settled there again. Witness then drew out the ramrod of his gun, and drove it down into the soft sandy earth at that spot; when he withdrew it the rod smelt offensively; witness plunged the ramrod down twice more, and the third time, feeling a hard body stop his ramrod, he twisted it round two or three times, and found on withdrawing it that the smell was not only worse, but a small piece of thread was hanging to it, similar to the threads in a blue shirt. Witness then went up the bank, and when Heeny arrived he sent him for a spade, and caused him to dig at that spot.

At about two feet they came on a short log, and having removed it they shortly arrived at a human body wrapped up in a sack, which and the shirt Henny cut open slightly, so that witness was satisfied it was a human body. Witness then left Heeny as guard over the body, after covering it up again, and started for Cassilis, but his horse failing he returned to the grave with Clarke whom he met. The next morning Clarke and Heeny again dug down to the body and exposed it sufficiently to satisfy them that it was the body of Palfrey. Having covered the body up, witness then rode to Cassilis, and informed the police who came, and Dr Nichol was sent for to examine the body.

This witness was again cross-examined at great length by Mr Purefoy with regards to his memory of the various conversations which he had detailed, but his evidence was not shaken except by mere verbal differences.

John Heeny corroborated the evidence of Mr Brady so far as he had been with him, and was also present when Dr Nichol examined the body found by Mr Brady, and which was Joseph Palfrey's.

Adolphus Bartley [Bartlett] Jones deposed that on the 25th or 26th May prisoner came to Reedy Creek, and reported the disappearance of Palfrey, telling witness that he had left home on the 15th, and that on the following Friday prisoner found his horse on the run without a bridle, but having a saddle and one stirrup on. Witness went to the station with prisoner to search for Palfrey and feeling suspicious of foul play having occurred, he the next day went to Cassilis to report it to the police. Witness then returned to the hut by another road, and found on his arrival that the police were there. Prisoner came in afterwards, and was apprehended by Chief Constable Kerr. Witness saw the tomahawk produced in Mr Kerr's possession, at the end of the hut. The saddle prisoner was riding on when he came to Reedy Creek, he told witness was the one Palfrey had ridden away on; it did not look torn or injured; witness would expect a horse to roll a good deal if it was in the bush for several days, which would injure the saddle more or less. Witness never saw prisoner and Palfrey quarrelling. When they returned from the search, before witness went to Cassilis, Purcell brought witness the tomahawk, and said, "This woman will soon find a plan to settle me." The tomahawk was dirty, and witness threw it from him. Other expressions might have been used by prisoner, but witness could not remember the exact words. Witness found a spur in the hut, and a whip, which witness knew belonged to Palfrey.

Thomas Clarke deposed that he was overseer to Mr Blackstone at Drummond's Flat, and that having heard of the disappearance of Palfrey he went to Purcell's hut, and remained some days, assisting in the search. During this time, he had several conversations with the prisoner, which he detailed in length. Having heard from him that the horse looked much rolled and fatigued on Friday, witness went to look at him on Tuesday, and found he looked fresh and sleek, without any appearance of having been ridden for some time. On Thursday Mrs Purcell in consequence of a conversation with witness, asked her husband for the tomahawk, which she had left lying on her boots; prisoner asked, "Why do you want to know?" and added, I know what you mean by the tomahawk; will you swear you put it there?" Prisoner, however, went out in a minute or two, and must have brought in the tomahawk, for witness saw it in his wife's hands immediately after, but noticed nothing particular about it.
Witness was present when the body was dug up by Mr Brady and Heeny, and recognised it, and saw the body afterwards again finally dug up, that Dr Nichol might examine it; it was the body of Joseph Palfrey.

Mr Purefoy cross-examined the witness at some length, and elicited that a few of the expressions he detailed had not been mentioned by him at the police office examinations.

Thomas Kerr deposed that he was Chief Constable of Cassilis, and that on receiving information he went to the prisoner's station; he was not at home, but came in the afternoon; witness apprehended him, and searched him, and found some papers and £19 in money on him. On witness entering the house he immediately examined all the tools in the house, and found the tomahawk produced; he examined it closely, and found on it a single hair, which he believed to be human, embedded in what appeared to him coagulated blood; the hair was still on it, but the blood looked more like rust now. (The tomahawk was handed to his Honour, and the jury, and the single hair was observed still adhering to it). It was a dark hair, similar to Palfrey's in colour and appearance. In the morning the prisoner claimed the pencil paper written by Mr Brady, which witness had found in prisoner's pocket, as being his wife's.

By Mr Purefoy Witness believed the hair to have been human, and the marks to be blood from their appearance.

Alfred John Nichol, surgeon, deposed that he resided at Cassilis, and went to prisoner's station early in June, where he examined the dead body of Joseph Palfrey The legs were doubled up in the sack when removed from the grave. Witness found no external appearance of injury on the head, but having opened it he found that the skull was fractured, by what appeared to be two heavy blows from a blunt instrument, the pieces of the skull being driven into the brain. Such an instrument as the tomahawk produced would cause such an injury, if the blows were struck with the blunt end of the head. There was no blood on the head or clothes, and decomposition had gone on to a considerable extent about the head and neck, but much less about the body. Witness did not open the body, but found no external marks of injury on it. There was a large depression on the head, but the skin was not cut, and there was no external injury. The fracture of the skull was the cause of death. Witness saw nothing particular about the tomahawk produced except the single hair attached to it, which appeared to be human hair, the marks on it might be coagulated blood, but he could not say they were without analysing them. Witness thought the body had been laying three weeks or more in the earth, which was sandy and dry; the clothing was very wet, much more so than was usual about a decomposing body.

By Mr Purefoy The contusions were on the right side of the head, approaching to the back and upper part of the skull; the decomposition prevented the witness's observing any marks of external haemorrhage; there must have been extensive external or internal haemorrhage; witness found no evidence of internal haemorrhage on opening the skull. There was no injury on the body, and witness did not examine the vital organs. Witness was positive the injuries on the skull were inflicted before death. He observed no suffusion of blood, no mass of coagulated blood and no serum. Witness certainly would expect extensive haemorrhage at the time of injury. The body was saturated by water; witness was not prepared to say to say that death was not caused by drowning; it was possible it might, but very improbable, and from the whole appearance witness had no doubt that death was caused by the fracture of the skull. Decomposition would have prevented to some extent the appearance of external injury, and had almost entirely removed the brain.

By the Court: The skin was in its natural state when witness examined the head, although the bone beneath had fallen into the cavity of the brain, so that the skin and bone had separated in the course of decomposition, and probably while they were removing the body. Witness thought death was undoubtedly caused by the fractured skull.
By a juror: Witness believed the single hair to be human, and thought it like Palfrey's.

This closed the case for the prosecution.

Mr Purefoy addressed the jury for the defence. There was no duty so serious as that in which they were all now engaged, as on the result of their inquiry the life of a fellow creature depended. His duty was to endeavour to prevent an innocent man being made to suffer for the foul crime of murder. But the evidence against his client was not only simply circumstantial, the most suspicious of all proof, but depending entirely on the reports of his expressions, conveyed to them, after interval of many months, by witnesses who themselves admitted they could not remember his exact words. And from such weak evidence they were called on to draw the inference that the prisoner was guilty of this crime. It was a case that called for the most deliberate investigation, for, beyond these expressions, there was not any evidence to connect the prisoner with the death of Palfrey, nor any evidence that he had ever seen him from the day when he was at Mrs McDonald's. In some cases, presumptive evidence was so strong that they could not avoid being convinced by it, but unless they could conclude not only that the prisoner may have committed the crime, but that Palfrey had died from violence, and that no one but the prisoner could have murdered him, they must acquit the prisoner, for God forbid that any man should be found guilty of such a crime on supposition. In this light, if any fact proved inconsistent with the idea of his guilt, then the whole case fell to the ground; and he felt sure that if they would attend to him carefully while he went over the evidence, they would acquit the prisoner. The learned gentleman then went through the evidence, particularly dwelling on the probability of Palfrey's death being caused by drowning, and that the injuries on the skull were caused by the dragging him from the water to his grave. He would call a medical man of undoubted skill who had heard the whole of the evidence, and who would tell them that the appearances found by Dr Nichol were altogether inconsistent with the belief that the blows were inflicted on Palfrey in life, and he rested confidently on their conclusion that the prisoner was not guilty of causing Palfrey's death as laid out in the indictment.

Michael McCartney deposed that he was a surgeon, practising in Maitland, it was very difficult to distinguish between fractures of the nature alluded to inflicted before death and shortly after death; if such wounds as described were inflicted in life he should expect external swelling, with suffusion of blood, and internal haemorrhage; if after death then he should look for none of these consequences unless the death had been caused by lightning; internal haemorrhage would be more especially follow from a fracture in the position described; decomposition, as described by Dr Nichols, had proceeded so far as to nearly remove the brain and all appearance of haemorrhage; witness should explain this by immersion after death, which would cause both appearances; it was not unusual for fractures of the skull to produce speedy decomposition of the brain; where there was no appearance of extravagation of blood a medical man would naturally conclude that the injury had been inflicted after death; if a man riding swiftly fell off his horse, and his skull came on a stone, it might produce such a fracture.

The Solicitor General replied.
His Honour charged the jury, dwelling on the solemn nature of the investigation, and having gone carefully through the whole of the evidence, he left it for them to decide.
The jury retired for a few minutes, and brought in a verdict of guilty, and the prisoner was remanded for sentence.

THE MURDER OF PALFREY

Maitland Mercury 18th September 1847

The whole of the jury who sat on the case of Purcell, convicted of the murder of Joseph Palfrey, having signed a memorial to his Honour, recommending the prisoner to mercy on the ground of gross provocation he had received, it was presented by the foreman.

His Honour having perused it, replied that he would lay the memorial before the executive, and the jury might rely that it would meet attentive consideration.

SENTENCE FOR MURDER

Maitland Mercury 29th September 1847

Before the Court, Monday 27th September 1847: John Purcell, convicted on Monday, the 13th September, of the murder of Joseph Palfrey was sentenced to death. His Honour said he had postponed until the last day of the Circuit Court the solemn and distressing duty of passing sentence of death on the prisoner. In most cases of crime, the judge was invested with the privilege of passing a severe or lenient sentence in proportion to the apparent heinousness of the offence; but in the cases of murder, the law allowed no such discretion, and he could only pass sentence of death where a prisoner was convicted of murder. In this case the evidence was circumstantial only, as was usually the case with crimes of so deep a dye that men naturally did their utmost to conceal their having committed them; but it was here aided by the repeated expressions of the prisoner, almost accounting to admissions. The almost miraculous manner in which the body of the murdered man had been discovered reminded him strongly of a case tried before himself at Maitland eighteen months since; and both cases illustrated the truth of the saying, that "Murder, though it hath no tongue, yet speaks with most miraculous organ." From all the circumstances, there could be little doubt that the victim had been taken unawares, and that the blow was as foul as it was fatal. It was of little avail for him, then, to dwell on the main topic of provocation, the suspected infidelity of the prisoner's wife; but it was remarkable that the murder was not committed under the sudden impulse of passion on discovering her infidelity, but took place long after it was known, or at any rate believed by the prisoner. Since the prisoner's trial, a memorial had been presented to himself from the jury, recommending the prisoner to mercy. This prerogative was vested in the head of the Executive government, not in himself, and he would lay the memorial before him. He could not, in that place, hold out any hopes of mercy, and he solemnly adjured the prisoner to prepare for another world; and if mercy should hereafter be extended to the prisoner, and his life be spared, he trusted that the lesson he had received would be a warning to him for the remainder of his life. The sentence of the Court was, that John Purcell be taken to the gaol whence he came, and that he be taken from thence at such a time and to such a place as his Excellency the Governor may appoint, and that he be hanged by the neck until his body be dead.

MITIGATION OF PURCELL'S SENTENCE

Maitland Mercury 10th November 1847

The sentence of death passed upon John Purcell, who was convicted at the late Maitland Assizes of the murder of Joseph Palfrey has been commuted to three years' hard labour in irons, and at the termination of that period to be transported for life.

Points for the reader to consider:

- James Brady reported supposed conversations with John Purcell that could not be verified by other persons. These conversations were to the detriment of Purcell.
- James Brady set up a sheep station over the land of Palfrey and Purcell as soon as Purcell was apprehended.
- Thomas Clark who examined the tomahawk could see no stain on it, but also stated his eye sight was not perfect. The Chief Constable noted a congealed substance with a hair stuck to the tomahawk even though it had been out in the rain.
- Purcell gave James Brady £19 which Brady claimed he gave to Purcell's wife.
- James Brady's description of finding the body of Palfrey appear neat and convenient, especially when there were no witnesses.
- Thomas Kerr stated that when he searched Purcell, he found £19 on him though Brady stated he gave the money to Purcell's wife.
- Why didn't Dr Nicol check the substance on the tomahawk to determine if it was blood?
- How did the clothes on the body become wet if the soil was dry?

- Why didn't the Dr examine the lungs for water?
- It is possible that Palfrey dived into the river and struck his head.
- Did James Brady have something to do with disposing of the body?

Both John and Bridget Purcell disappear from the records following the trial.

CASE 11 - 1847 **RAVENSWORTH**

BERNARD FOX **DECEASED VICTIM (Sheep overseer at Ravensworth Station)**

CHARLES COOPER **ACCUSED WITH MURDER (TL holder at Ravensworth Station)**

PERSONS FOR THE PROSECUTION

John Carlyle	**storekeeper for Edward Bowman, Ravensworth Station**
George Shearer	**cook at Ravensworth Station**
Theophilus Cooper	**son of Rev Cooper, residing at Ravensworth Station**
William Haydon	**in the service of Edward Bowman**
Dr Henry Glennie	**surgeon, lived at Dulwich**

PERSONS FOR THE DEFENCE

Nil, barristers had left Maitland for the day and witnesses requested by accused were not subpoenaed. The trial proceeded without them.

Maitland Mercury 30th October 1847

Charles Cooper, a ticket-of-leave holder was charged with the wilful murder of Bernard Fox a sheep overseer, at Ravensworth on the night of the 25th instant. The prisoner was heavily ironed, and appeared to be deeply affected at the awful situation in which he was placed.

John Carlyle, who is a storekeeper on the establishment of Mr Edward Bowman, at Ravensworth deposed that on the night in question he was returning to the farm, when he met the prisoner, who asked him if he was Mr Carlyle upon his replying that he was, he (prisoner) complained about some rations and said that he had none. Witness told him that he had sent out a fortnight's rations. (Prisoner was stationed at Falbrook). Prisoner then got rather abusive, and Witness walked away, telling him that if he wished for anymore, he (prisoner) must apply to Mr Bowman. Witness then walked into the cottage and into his room. Prisoner followed towards the corner of the fence. While witness was washing his hands, he heard prisoner and deceased quarrelling, and heard the prisoner use the words "b--- liar." Witness then heard some scuffling and looking through the window, saw the prisoner and deceased struggling together outside the fence. Witness then ran out of his room towards the cottage gate, just as the prisoner and deceased parted. Witness then told prisoner to go to his station, as he wished to hear no more of this. Deceased was then standing in a stooping posture with his hands on the lower part of his stomach, and cried out, "he has something in his hand, he has a knife." Deceased then pressed his side harder, and said, "Oh my God! The villain has stabbed me – I am killed – I am done for."

Witness saw Fox into the house and while he was going out George Shearer rushed past witness, with something in his hand; he seemed as if he was going to strike the prisoner and said, "You've stabbed the man." Prisoner answered, "I would stab you, or anyone that would take his part," or words to that effect. Witness then passed between prisoner and Shearer and went to the house and informed Mr Bowman what had happened, who sent a man off for Dr Glennie.

The man Bernard Fox had since died. Witness did not know of any previous quarrel between the prisoner and Fox The deceased was a sheep overseer and was over the prisoner, who was a watchman.

George Shearer, a cook at Ravensworth deposed that on Monday the 25th instant, after dark, prisoner passed his kitchen with the former witness. They were having words about rations. Mr Carlyle told the prisoner to go to Mr Bowman, as he would have nothing to do with him. Prisoner still followed Mr Carlyle as if he intended to strike him. Bernard Fox was then in the kitchen and had just had his dinner. Witness asked deceased to come with him, as he (witness) thought that prisoner would rush Carlyle and they had better go out to save him. Fox went out and said to the prisoner, "You scoundrel, what noise is this you are making? You are not due for rations." Prisoner then came up to Fox and asked him, "What have you got to do with it?" and they both met and struck blows on both sides. Fox had hold of prisoner by the shirt or handkerchief, witness could not tell which, as it was dark.

Deceased then let go his hold and said, "The villain has a knife in his hand." Fox then roared out, "I am done" and made for the cottage and fell on the floor. Witness then examined him and found blood on his stomach and that he was stabbed. Witness took up a fire shovel and ran out the gate where he saw prisoner and said "You villain, you have stabbed the man." Prisoner said, "Yes and I'll stab you too, or any wretch that take his part." Witness told prisoner that he would do his best to take him, when he saw Mr Cooper and Mr Carlyle approaching the gate and prisoner then ran off as hard as he could. Witness did not know which struck the first blow as it was in the dark; the one appeared as eager for the scuffle as the other; deceased was a quiet man.

Theophilus Cooper, son of the Rev. Cooper, deposed that he resided at Ravensworth. On Monday last, about eight in the evening, witness was coming down from the cottage at Ravensworth, when he heard high words between the prisoner and someone else. Witness went to the cottage and saw prisoner and deceased struggling together. Witness did not think the struggle lasted more than a minute or two when deceased rushed away from prisoner and said, "The villain has got something in his hand." He stooped down and said, "He has got a knife in his hand", deceased then placed his hand to his side and said, "I'm stabbed, I'm done, I'm done." Deceased then staggered into the cottage, witness followed him and saw Shearer run out with a fire shovel in his hand. The time witness saw deceased put his hand to his side he observed prisoner make a motion with his hand, as if he was putting something in his pocket.

William Haydon deposed that he was in the service of Mr Edward Bowman, at Ravensworth. On Monday evening last witness was at the hut where prisoner was stopping. Prisoner got up to go home, when witness asked him where he was going, prisoner answered that he was going to have a b----y row. Prisoner then went away in the direction of the cottage.

Dr Henry Glennie deposed to having been sent for to Ravensworth to attend to deceased. Deceased had been wounded in two places by a sharp instrument; one of the cuts had penetrated the stomach; he had also made a post mortem examination and found that death had been caused by these wounds.
Other evidence was also heard, which corroborated the former.
The prisoner having been called on for his defence declined saying anything and was fully committed to take his trial for the murder.

Case of Murder, Maitland Circuit Court
Before his Honour the Chief Justice
Maitland Mercury, Tuesday 15th February 1848

Charles Cooper was indicted for murdering Bernard Fox at Ravensworth by striking him on the belly with a knife on the 25th October 1847 and inflicting wounds whereof he died on the 26th October.

The prisoner had applied to his Honour to be allowed counsel for his defence, but the application not having been made until the barristers had left Maitland, the request could not be complied with. The prisoner then enquired whether three witnesses he had subpoenaed were in attendance; it turned out they were not, but it was stated that their evidence could not be material, and the prisoner had not applied to have them heard before the magistrates, his Honour refused to postpone the trial. His Honour, however, added publicly, that as so much difficulty was thrown in the way of poor prisoners' procuring witnesses, in order to avoid a slight expense to the country, he should make an invariable rule of postponing a trial when it was proved that witnesses for the prisoner were not in attendance, whom he had wished to call before the magistrates and whose evidence was on affidavit to be material, but that it was necessary that the prisoner should have called them, or desired them to be called, before the magistrates at his committal.

The trial then proceeded and the Solicitor General having stated the case to the jury, called:

Peter Haydon, who deposed that on the evening of the 25th October prisoner left his hut on the Ravensworth estate, saying he was going to have a bloody row. He went away in the direction of the cottage in which Mr Carlyle and the two Messrs Cooper lived. Mr Carlyle was the storekeeper and prisoner was a watchman; deceased was an overseer who lived near the cottage. Witness never heard of any quarrel between prisoner and the deceased. Prisoner bore the character of being a quarrelsome man.

John Carlyle deposed that prisoner met him a short distance from the cottage and complained about his rations. Witness told him he had sent them and if prisoner wanted more he must go to Mr Bowman. Prisoner commenced abusing him, but witness walked away and went into the cottage. Shortly after witness heard Fox and prisoner having words, followed by the sound of scuffing, witness looked out the window and saw the prisoner and Fox struggling together. Witness ran out and when he got out, they had parted, prisoner still being about the same place, but Fox two or three yards off, in a stooping posture, holding his hands on his belly. Fox cried out, "Oh my God, the villain has stabbed me, I'm killed, I'm done for." Witness assisted Fox into the cottage and a man named George Shearer went up to prisoner and accused him of having stabbed Fox Prisoner replied that he would stab

him or any other man who would take his part. Witness went and informed Mr Bowman. Dr Glennie was sent for who attended Fox till his death, which took place the next evening.
In cross-examination the prisoner endeavoured to show that he was short of rations and that Fox had abused and struck him first.

George Shearer deposed that he saw prisoner and Mr Carlyle having words; when Mr Carlyle turned away and came to the cottage, prisoner came quickly after him to the door, witness thought he was going to strike Mr Carlyle. Witness asked Fox who was dining with witness in the kitchen to go out with him to prevent it. They went out, Fox and the prisoner had some words and then commenced fighting. They fought for about two minutes, when Fox drew back, putting his hands on his stomach, and said, "I am stabbed, the villain has got a knife in his hand; I'm done, I'm a dead man. Witness assisted Fox into the cottage and saw a wound on the left side of his stomach, which was bleeding freely. Witness went out with a shovel and accused prisoner of having stabbed Fox Prisoner said, "Yes, and I'll stab you too or any bloody wretch who will take his part." Fox was a quiet inoffensive man. Fox did not knock the prisoner down.

Theophilus Cooper deposed that he came up as the struggle was going on and it only lasted about a minute more, after which Fox drew back and exclaimed that he was stabbed. This witness corroborated the previous evidence.

Samuel Swain apprehended prisoner about four miles from the cottage, shortly after the occurrence. Mr Bowman and the gardener accompanied witness to apprehend him.

Dr Glennie deposed that he found two wounds on the body of Fox, one a light wound under the left arm, and the second a deep wound on the upper part of the abdomen. The second wound had penetrated the stomach and witness found on making a post mortem examination that it had caused death. The wounds were such as would have been inflicted by a knife.

The prisoner, who had in cross-examination accused all the witnesses, except Dr Glennie, of speaking falsely, put in a written defence, denying having committed the crime. His Honour had at considerable length cross-examined the witnesses on behalf of the prisoner.

His Honour, in charging the jury, told them they must be satisfied that the prisoner had inflicted the wounds, intending to take life, before they could find him guilty of murder; insomuch as it was proved that Fox went to seek the quarrel himself. If they were of opinion, therefore, that he had no intention to take life, but had struck the blow, which led to the death of Fox they would find him guilty of manslaughter. If they thought the evidence insufficient to prove that the prisoner did stab Fox, they would acquit him.

The jury retired for an hour and then returned with a verdict of guilty of manslaughter. The prisoner was sentenced to hard labour on the roads or public works for ten years, the first three years in irons[26].

Some thoughts:

- The prisoner had applied to his Honour to be allowed counsel for his defence, but the application not having been made until the barristers had left Maitland, the request could not be complied with. The prisoner then enquired whether three witnesses he had subpoenaed were in attendance; it turned out they were not, but it was stated that their evidence could not be material, and the prisoner had not applied to have them heard before the magistrates, his Honour refused to postpone the trial.
- This certainly placed the prisoner at a disadvantage.
- The jury found him not guilty of murder, but of manslaughter, this decision based on the evidence presented at this trial, I believe was which was the correct decision.

Bernard Fox was buried on the top of a ridge overlooking St Clements C of E Church, Camberwell. Someone arranged for the erection of a headstone.

CASE 12 - 1848 **MUSWELLBROOK**

RICHARD CONNOLLY **DECEASED VICTIM**

GEORGE WATERS WARD **ACCUSED MURDERER**

PERSONS FOR THE PROSECUTION

Thomas White	**lived at Woolaman, station owner by Dr Jenkins**
Michael Riley	**shepherd employed by Mrs White, station beyond**
Samuel Caldwell	**Aberdeen publican, Albert Hotel, Aberdeen**
George Lewis	**Muswellbrook**
John Thomas Baker	**employed by Dr Jenkins, Woolaman**
Thomas Maguire	**labourer employed by Mrs White**
Edward Avery	**bullock driver**
Thomas Ward	**bullock driver**
Charles Fox	**Chief Constable, Muswellbrook**
Thomas Fowler	**surgeon**
William Ryan	**farmer, Miller's Forest near Maitland**
Samuel Holt	**Chief Constable, Newcastle**

PERSONS FOR THE DEFENCE
Mr Purefoy
Mr Ward

This is a long and involved case. You, the reader, as a member of the jury will have to pay very close attention to the testimony of the persons giving evidence for the prosecution. There are a number of people involved and at times the evidence is contradictory. There is one person who is evasive regarding what he was doing in the vicinity of the murder scene.

Again, most of the information is taken directly from the newspapers of the time.

George Waters Ward, the accused man was apprehended in Newcastle and brought back to Muswellbrook for examination, following which he was committed to take his trial for murder at a higher court.

The case featured in the newspapers for a period of almost 12 months, an unusually long time in that era.

MURDER NEAR MUSWELLBROOK
Maitland Mercury 19th April 1848

Last Friday morning, as Chief Constable Fox of Muswellbrook, was returning home from the Quarter Sessions, he was hailed near Muswellbrook by a bullock-driver, who told him he had just discovered a man lying dead in the bush, who had evidently been murdered. Mr Fox went into the bush with the bullock-driver and in a gully, he found the body of a young man lying covered over with a rug and some branches. The body was lying in a pool of blood, the head being completely smashed in. From the spot where it was found, Mr Fox traced the track along which the body had been dragged, till he reached a place where a fire had been made, as if the deceased had camped there, and on the extinguished fire he observed a coat and hat lying partly consumed.

Further inquiries were made, and Mr Fox ascertained that two men had a day or two previously stopped at the Aberdeen Inn and Mr Caldwell, the landlord, having viewed the body, at once recognised it as being that of one of those two men. While at Mr Caldwell's he noticed that this unfortunate man, called by his companion Conolly[17] or Condon, had on his person a gold watch, and two silver watches, as well as several orders and cheques. Conolly had presented a cheque for £5 to Mr Caldwell in payment, but something about it or the men induced him to refuse it, and he was otherwise paid. Fox without delay traced a man answering the description of Conolly's companion down to Maitland, and from thence to Morpeth, which latter place he is supposed to have left by land on Monday morning, in the direction of Newcastle. Up to sunset last evening, no further trace of his movements had been found, but Mr Fox is still on the lookout for him. Whether, when found, he will prove to be one of the two men who were together at Aberdeen Inn remains to be seen.

[17] Various spellings in reports

MURDER NEAR MUSWELLBROOK

Maitland Mercury 22nd April 1848

On Tuesday evening, last the man supposed to be the murderer was seen twice in East Maitland; on the first occasion early in the evening, when he called at a store to purchase powder and buckshot, but bolted on observing that a man had left the shop. and ran as hard as he could for the bush; and on the second occasion about eleven o'clock, when he called at a public-house to light his pipe, and immediately decamped. On both occasions, his appearance induced parties to go for the police, but he got clear off each time. He is supposed to be still lurking about Maitland, or to have gone in the direction of Wollombi. The mounted police, who, with Chief Constable Fox, and some Maitland police, have been engaged in searching for him, are still doing so. Since we published the account in our last, we have gathered a few further particulars of the case.

It appears that Chief Constable Fox met the bullock-driver on Friday evening, the 14th, about a mile from Muswellbrook, and was taken by him to a waterhole in a small gully, where Mr Fox found the murdered man lying on his face, with his hands crossed over the top of his head. The back of his skull was beaten in, and there were also three holes made in it, one over the right eye, one behind and in front of the right ear. The body had evidently been dragged to this spot from the fire-place, along a small creek, and blood was seen on the grass near the fireplace.

The body was afterwards identified by a man named Baker as being that of Richard Connolly a man whom he had known in the service of Dr Jenkins; and Mr Caldwell identified him as one of two men who had stopped at his inn on the previous Wednesday. On Saturday morning Mr Fox received a letter from Dr Jenkins, informing him that Connolly had absconded from his service, taking with him, as he suspected, a gold watch, and he believed he had been induced to abscond by a man, a shipmate of Connolly's, who had visited the station. Dr J described the men, and directed Mr Fox to apprehend Connolly if he met with him. Mr Caldwell stated that Connolly and another man called at his house on Wednesday, and dined and shaved themselves. Mr Caldwell heard them talking about a gold watch, and saw two silver watches in their possession. They changed a cheque of Dr Jenkins's with him, and he saw that they had a similar cheque. The second man is described as a square-built active young man, about thirty years of age, dark complexion, and dark hair, with full dark whiskers coming low under the chin, but not meeting; when at Mr Caldwell's he was dressed in dark fustian trousers, stripped shirt, and low-crowned cabbage tree hat, and carried a square bundle in a handkerchief. Immediately on hearing of the murder, Lieutenant O'Connell with a party of mounted police, proceeded to the spot, and traced such a man to Maitland, where they arrived late on Saturday evening. They continued the search on Sunday without success, and on Sunday evening, Chief Constable Fox also arrived, having also traced the man down to Maitland. During Sunday morning two of the Maitland police met the man, but they had unfortunately not then heard a word of the murder, and the man has not since been seen by any of the police, although he was in a house in Morpeth on Monday morning, and in two others, as already related, on Tuesday.

THE MUSWELLBROOK MURDER

Maitland Mercury 6th May 1848

The man apprehended at Newcastle on Tuesday the 25th ultimo, by Chief Constable Holt on suspicion of being the murderer of Richard Connolly (or rather John Connolly, as known in Dr Jenkins' service), has acknowledged to having been in company with Connolly at the Aberdeen Inn. He is now on his way to Muswellbrook, having been forwarded from Newcastle to Maitland on Thursday, and sent on from this place yesterday morning under escort. He first gave his name as George Ward to Mr Holt, but afterwards told the Newcastle bench that his name was George Waters Ward, and that he came to the colony a free man. From information received by Dr Jenkins his real name is supposed to be George Newman, and he is believed to have come to the colony a prisoner in 1829, as George Waters, alias Newman. He has been recognised by the Maitland police as being the man whom they and the mounted police were in pursuit of about the 15th to the 18th April, having met by two of the police before they had heard of the murder.

Dr Jenkins, in forwarding to Muswellbrook bench what information he had obtained, stated that Connolly, when he left, had with him in addition to Dr J's gold and silver watches, a silver watch of his own, without the second hand, and that parties who had known Newman were aware that he had lived some time in and near Parramatta, part of the time as gardener at Mr Lawson's of Prospect.

Yesterday, a settler named William Ryan residing at Miller's Forest, appeared voluntarily before the Maitland bench, and gave up a watch he had bought from a man who gave his name as George Hucas. Ryan deposed that

Hucas came to his house about dusk on Sunday, the 16th April, asking for employment, stating that he had been recommended to apply to him by the puntman at Raymond Terrace. Ryan hired him at 8s per week. Hucas remained with him until Sunday following, when he left to go to Raymond Terrace, after which Ryan saw no more of him. Hucas told Ryan he had served his time with Mr Lawson, and had a discharge from a person at Prospect. During the time Hucas remained at Ryan's, he sold him a silver watch, without a second hand, with a brass key fastened to a plaited string; the number 2593 scratched on the inside, maker's name 'Robert, Geneva,' on the dial and on the inside also. Hucas was not paid by Mr Ryan nor did he ask for payment. Hucas also left at Mr Ryan's a light tweed coat, and it seems singular that he neither took it, nor asked for payment for the watch, when he left for Raymond Terrace.

Last evening a mate of Connolly's on Dr Jenkins' station arrived in Maitland by the mail, and informed police that Ward, alias Newman, whom he met on the road in charge of the stables, was the man in whose company Connolly absconded from the station, and the coat left by Hucas at Mr Ryan's was the coat the man was carrying; he thought the watch sold by Hucas was like Connolly's watch, but could not swear to it. There is now, therefore, no doubt that Connolly's companion is in custody.

THE RECENT MURDER
Maitland Mercury 10th May 1848

There is every reason to believe that the man apprehended at Newcastle is the man who was in company with the murdered man, Connolly; he is expected to arrive in Muswellbrook this evening.

POLICE COURT, MUSWELLBROOK-MURDER OF CONNOLLY
Maitland Mercury 24th May 1848

George Waters Ward was, on Monday the 22nd May, fully committed by Captain Wright JP, to take his trial for the wilful murder of Richard Connolly.

The following was the evidence taken at the examination:

Chief Constable Fox being sworn, deposed: On Tuesday, the 14th April last, I was returning home from Maitland Quarter Sessions; I was at Bowman's Creek, 10 miles from Muswellbrook, about 12 0'clock that day, when I meet the prisoner. He was crossing the water as I was going down the creek; he passed me at in a fast-walking pace a short distance, and turned around and asked me how far it was to Patrick's Plains. I told him eleven miles; he then went towards Singleton and I towards Muswellbrook. I arrived within a mile of Muswellbrook about sundown, when I was shown the body of a dead man, laying in Muswell Brook Creek, by a man by the named Ahrey[18] who said he had not been nearer the body than the bank of the creek, which was about ten yards. I searched previous to going near the body, to see if I could find any foot-marks. I found the print of a naked foot, very plain, in the sand. I have measured the prisoner's foot and it corresponds with the foot-mark I found. After removing a dark rug that covered a portion of the body and a cap that was on the head, I saw the back part of the head had been broken in, apparently with an axe or tomahawk, or a very sharp-edged stone. There was a hole in the side of the head and a hole in the temple, and over the eye, and several other cuts about the head.

After the Doctor had examined the body I removed it to the Court-house; it was then after dark. The red cap was evidently placed on the head after the murder had been committed, as there were no holes in. Next morning I went out to where I brought the body from, and found the track where the body had been dragged along the ground to where it lay, from a log about 200 yards off where a fire had been. In searching the ashes, I found part of a drab coat, clotted with blood, partly burnt, also a cabbage-tree hat part burnt, and a pint pot, with a tree scratched on the bottom of it and wrote under, 'Tree of Knowledge'. A spot of ground close to the ashes, about nine inches in diameter, was covered in blood.

I have shown the silver watch I now produce to the prisoner, and asked him if he knew it, he said he knew it well, it was his property, but it was Connolly's watch, and he brought it from him at the Aberdeen Inn when he was in company with him there. I also showed prisoner the coat I now produce, and he said it was his, and he could give a very good account how he came by it. John T Baker has seen the coat, and says that the coat was once his property, but that he sold it to Connolly whose dead body he saw on the 15th April last, in this Court-house, murdered.

---

[18] Also spelt Avery

R L Jenkins, surgeon, of Peel River, being sworn, deposed: Richard Connolly, who I am informed, is murdered, was in my employ, but absconded. The watch now produced I can positively swear was Connolly's; I gave it to him myself after getting it repaired for him in Sydney, the account I now produce. I received from the watchmaker, who repaired it, with the description and number of the watch wrote on it.

John T Baker, residing at Muswellbrook, being sworn, deposed: The coat now produced was my property, but I sold it to Richard Connolly for one pound, whose dead body I identified at this Court-house on 15th April last, the day he was found murdered.

George Lewis of Muswellbrook, being sworn, deposed: On Wednesday, 12th April last, I was at the Aberdeen Inn I saw the prisoner in company with another man there. I believe the man I saw dead in this Court-house on the following Saturday was the other man, who wore a coat of the same description as the one now produced, but I think it has been since washed.

Samuel Caldwell, inn-keeper at Aberdeen, being sworn, deposed: I recollect the prisoner at the bar, and Richard Connolly, being at my house on the 12th April last; they had dinner together; in the afternoon Connolly came to my counter and pulled out his watch, and asked me to regulate it for him by my clock; the watch now produced is exactly like it; it wanted the second hand, the same as this watch. Connolly also pulled out a second watch, which was very much out of repair, the hand was broke off. The second watch now produced is exactly like the watch. Connolly put both watches in his pocket. Connolly worn a tweed coat, it had no buttons, and the pockets were sideways near the front; the coat now produced is of the very same description. The prisoner and Connolly left my house in company together, about half-past 8 o'clock, to go towards Muswellbrook. They were both perfectly sober.

MUSWELL BROOK, THE LATE MURDER
Maitland Mercury 22nd July 1848

The following additional and material evidence has been given against the man George Waters Ward committed in May last to take his trial at the ensuing Assizes for the wilful murder of Richard Connolly, near Muswellbrook.

Police Court, Friday 14th July 1848: It appeared from the evidence of Chief Constable Fox that, as he was returning home yesterday from the Maitland Quarter Sessions, he was accompanied part of the way by a man named Thomas Maguire. When passing Bowman's Creek Mr Fox told Maguire it was in that creek, he met the man that was committed for the late murder near Muswellbrook, as he was returning from the last April Quarter Sessions.

Maguire then said he was he had been into Muswellbrook about that time, and he was returning home on Wednesday night, the 12th April last, and came about a mile on the Singleton Road, then lay down under a tree, but soon arose, and went a little distance off came up to a fire in the bush. Maguire asked them how far they came; they said not far that night, but did not say from where. After some conversation, he said it was about 12 o'clock, and one of them lay down, and said they would stop there until morning. Maguire asked them why they did not stop in Muswellbrook, one of them replied the houses were all shut up as they came through, and foot travellers could lodge anywhere. Maguire soon after left to go home, and went about three miles on the road, and lay down again from the effects of a headache he had. When he arose, he found that he had left his bundle where he was laying in the bush near Muswellbrook. He went back to search for it, and afterwards went over to the fire to light his pipe, where he left the two men at camp and found that the men were gone. Saw that there was burning in the fire what Maguire thought was a lot of rags or something of that sort.

Maguire described one of the men as about 5 feet 6 or 7 inches, stoutish made, full of face, with very large black whiskers, and wearing a rough, light-coloured drab coat and said he would know the man very well again if he saw him. The other man he described as having no whiskers, and sandy hair, about 5 feet 6 inches. Maguire lives at a station about ten miles from Muswellbrook, on the old Singleton Road.

Mr Fox requested him to ride on with him that night to Muswellbrook, and show him the place where he saw the two men at camp, and the rags burning in the fire after they were gone. He did so; but Mr Fox states that it was with very much reluctance that Maguire came to give evidence of what he had told him. The Chief Constable positively swears that the place pointed out to him by Maguire was the very identical spot where Connelly was murdered on the night of the 12th or 13th of April, and where he, Mr F found in the fire ashes, partly burnt, on the morning of the 15th April last, after finding the murdered body, the remains of a rough, light-coloured drab coat, clotted with blood. Mr Fox, further states that one of the descriptions given by Maguire of the men answers that of George Waters Ward the man committed for the murder, and the other answers that of the deceased, Connelly. Maguire was detained until court-time next morning, and then gave evidence corroborating the Chief Constable's statement; and further deposed that he had heard of the murder about the time it occurred, but did not know exactly when or where, or how it happened, and that he had no opportunity of making this evidence known previous to his conversation with Mr Fox about the murder yesterday, when accidentally travelling with him. It will be in the recollection of the readers of your Journal that although Connolly's two watches and coat were traced to Ward, no witnesses, previous to Maguire had seen him nearer Muswellbrook than Aberdeen 9 miles off, and Bowman's Creek, 18 miles off, from where the murder was committed.

WILFUL MURDER, MAITLAND CIRCUIT COURT
Maitland Mercury 16th September 1848

George Waters Ward was indicted for having, at Muswellbrook Creek, on 12th April 1848, feloniously assaulted one Richard Connolly otherwise Richard King, and for having with a certain unknown blunt instrument, held in both his hands, on the left side of the head and on the front of the head of the said Richard Connolly inflicted divers mortal wounds and bruises, whereof the said Richard Connolly did instantly die, and that thus he, the said George Waters Ward did feloniously kill and murder the said Richard Connolly. In a second count, the wounds were said to have been inflicted, and the murder committed, by an axe, held in both hands of the said George Waters Ward.

Ward applied for a postponement of his trial to the next Circuit Court, on the ground that two material witnesses for his defence were absent.

He was ordered to renew the application on affidavit on the following morning, and was removed from the bar.

George Waters Ward who had been arraigned on Thursday for the murder of Richard Connolly at Muswell Brook Creek, on the 12th April 1848, and who had then applied for a postponement of his trial, was brought up and informed that his trial was postponed till the next Circuit Court, the Attorney General also wishing to have it postponed.

Muswellbrook Police Court. The Late Murder
Maitland Mercury 4th November 1848

Chief Constable Fox has brought forward further evidence relative to the murder of Connelly, corroborating the evidence of Thomas McGuire, who has identified George Waters Ward as one of two men that camped at the fire where the murder was committed on the night of the 12th April last. It appeared from the evidence of Patrick Burns who is the father of a family, and in charge of the station where McGuire resided. McGuire went into Muswellbrook in April last, and that he returned home to the station a little before daylight on the morning of the 13th April, this being the morning after the murder. Burns, asking him the reason of his being absent from the station so long, McGuire then related to him the same circumstances as detailed in his evidence. Being to his leaving two men at the fire about 12 o'clock at night, and his returning to the fire two hours before daylight and finding that the two men were then gone, the particulars of which appeared in your journal of July last.

WILFUL MURDER, MAITLAND CIRCUIT COURT
Maitland Mercury 14th February 1849

George Waters Ward was indicted for having, at Muswellbrook Creek, on 12th April 1848, feloniously assaulted one Richard Connolly, otherwise Richard King, and for having with a certain unknown blunt instrument, held in both his hands, on the left side of the head and on the front of the head of the said Richard Connolly inflicted divers mortal wounds and bruises, whereof the said Richard Connolly did instantly die, and that thus he, the said George Waters Ward did feloniously kill and murder the said Richard Connolly. In a second count, the wounds were said to have been inflicted, and the murder committed, by an axe, held in both hands of the said George Waters Ward.

Mr Purefoy at the request of his Honour, undertook to watch the evidence on behalf of the prisoner; and Mr Ward also consented to act as attorney for the prisoner. By coincident, the defendant, George Waters Ward was being defended by Mr Purefoy, barrister and Mr Ward, attorney.

The Solicitor General stated the particulars of the case to the jury, urging them if they felt any reasonable doubt of the prisoner's guilt to give him the benefit of it.

Thomas White deposed that in April 1848 he lived at Woolaman, Dr Jenkins' station. Richard King, commonly called Richard Connolly, also lived there then. The prisoner was at the station on the 10th April, and was present when Connolly, witness and three or four others were at breakfast together; from their conversation it appeared that Connolly and prisoner had been acquainted in Van Dieman's Land, and after they had had some private conversation the prisoner went away, telling witness that he was going straight back to Sydney. Witness and Connolly went out to work, but about two o'clock Connolly left the station also, and witness had never seen him since. When Connolly left, he was dressed in a drab tweed coat and cabbage tree hat. He wrapped up in an opossum cloak some tea, sugar and tobacco, two check shirts, two Guernsey shirts, a pint and a quart pot, the tweed coat had no buttons behind and the pint pot had a tree marked on the bottom. The tweed coat produced he believed to be the one Connolly wore when he left and the pint pot produced, he believed to be the one Connolly wrapped up, and it had a tree like that one on the bottom. Connolly had with him a silver watch, which he had bought from another shepherd, who had entrusted it to Dr Jenkins to get repaired in Sydney.

Michael Riley deposed that he was a shepherd in April 1848, he was in the employ of Mrs White, at a station beyond Aberdeen. One evening, about that time, two men came to him and asked if they could stop the night, which witness consented to; one of the men, witness believed was the prisoner, but he could not say so positively, although he had no doubt of it. With this man, witness had no dealings, although that man offered him a rug, but with his companion, witness had dealings, giving him a coat for an opossum cloak, and an old watch for some guernsey and common shirts; the coat was the same colour and quality as the remnants produced, and it had a large cape. The watch wanted the glass, but witness could not say that he should know it again.

Samuel Caldwell deposed that he kept the Albert Hotel at Aberdeen. On the 12th April about one or two o'clock in the day, the prisoner and Richard Connolly came to witness's house, and called for dinner, which they had, they remained in the house till evening. While there, witness saw that Connolly had two watches with him, and witness had them some time in his hands. The watches produced were the same to the best of witness's belief. Connolly had a light tweed coat on exactly corresponding with the one produced. Connolly said he was going on to Muswellbrook and prisoner remarked that he wished to go there to see a man named George Lewis, who had dined with them, as he thought he could engage with him for a job of sawing. Connolly and the prisoner left witness's house about seven or eight o'clock in the evening, half or three-quarters of an hour after Lewis had left. Connolly had stopped at witness's house before, and gave his name as Richard Connolly. Witness had never seen the prisoner before that day.

George Lewis deposed that he took a meal at Mr Caldwell's on the evening of the 12th April in company with two men. Prisoner was one of them and a man who was spoken to as Connolly or Connell was the other. The prisoner was taking of hiring with witness, but did not do so. Witness left before the men left and never saw the prisoner after till he saw him in custody. Witness afterwards saw at the courthouse at Muswellbrook the dead body of a man whom he believed to be the man Connolly or Connell, but whose head was so mangled that he could not swear to him. That was on the 14th, witness believed; witness had no doubt it was his body.

John Thomas Baker deposed that in January 1848, he was in the employ of Dr Jenkins at Woolaman. Richard Connolly was also there. In the latter end of 1847 witness had sold to Connolly a tweed coat that had been made for witness. Witness removed to Muswellbrook, leaving Connolly at Woolaman. In April on Saturday the 15th, witness believed he saw the dead body of Connolly in the courthouse at Muswellbrook. He was positive it was his body. The coat produced was the coat witness sold to Connolly

Thomas Maguire deposed that he was in April last, a labourer in the employ of Mrs White. On Wednesday the 12th April, he left Muswellbrook to go home. He felt ill and lay down about ten o'clock in the morning and slept till four o'clock in the afternoon. Witness again went to sleep, and woke up in the night, at what hour he could not say, but it was dark. Witness then observed a fire on the opposite side of the road and going to it, he was about lighting his pipe, when two men came up from the direction of Muswellbrook, which was about a mile off. One of the men was the prisoner. Witness asked how far they were going and prisoner said not far. Witness remained at the fire about five minutes longer and then left, leaving the prisoner laying down and the other man making up the fire. Witness went on about a mile and getting ill again, he went to sleep. When he woke up, he walked on about two miles when he missed a bundle he had been carrying. Witness returned to the fire to look for it and when he got there noticed that there were some rags on the fire, but both men were gone. Witness lit his pipe and left in about a minute not having found his bundle. Witness never saw the prisoner before that night, but he was positive he was one of the two men, although there was now a difference in his appearance. There was a creek near the fire, called Muswellbrook Creek.

This witness was cross-examined at great length as to what made him so positive that the prisoner was one of the two men.

Edward Avery deposed that he was coming down country with drays, in company with Thomas Ward and encamped on the 14th April in the afternoon alongside Muswell Brook Creek about a mile from Muswellbrook. While looking for a place for their bullocks they noticed something in a shallow waterhole, which they found was the dead body of a man. They went and reported the fact to the magistrates and afterwards took Chief Constable Fox to the spot. The body was removed to Muswellbrook Court-house the same night.

Thomas Ward corroborated this evidence.

Charles Fox, Chief Constable of Muswellbrook, deposed that on being taken to the spot by the two last witnesses, he found the body lying on the face in a shallow waterhole; it was covered over with a dark rug, and on lifting it off witness saw a red cap on the head. Witness took this off and then saw that the back of the skull had been beaten in and also the side of the head. There was a shirt rolled round the neck, but otherwise the body was naked.

Witness removed the body to Muswellbrook Courthouse the same evening. The next morning witness tracked from the spot, a track as if the body had been dragged to the waterhole. The track led to a place where there had been a fire. By the ashes was a pool of blood about the size of the crown of a hat and in the ashes witness found the remains of a hat and a shepherd's tweed coat and a tin pot, the remnants produced and the pint pot were the same. Many persons in Muswellbrook Courthouse and amongst others, by Lewis, examined the body.

Before meeting Avery and Ward witness had met the prisoner, at an earlier hour on the same day. He met him at Bowman's Creek, nineteen miles from Muswellbrook and eleven from Singleton. After passing prisoner turned round to ask the distance to Patrick's Plains (Singleton), which witness told him and they parted, prisoner going on towards Singleton.

George Lewis recalled: Witness was present when Dr Fowler examined the body of the man Connolly or Connell; could not say on what day.

Thomas Fowler deposed that he was a surgeon and examined a body at the Muswellbrook Courthouse. Witness found a wound on the left temple and another on the back of the head. Either would have caused death if inflicted during life. The wound on the temple had been inflicted by some sharp instrument and the wound on the back of the head by a blunt instrument. Blows with a tomahawk would have caused such wounds; blows with an axe might have done so. Both or either of those wounds would have caused death. Witness believed them to have been inflicted before death from the extent of the extravasation[19] on the brain.

John Thomas Baker was recalled and deposed that he was present when Dr Fowler examined the body of Richard Connolly.

William Ryan deposed that he was a farmer, residing at Miller's Forest, below Maitland and that on Sunday the 16th April prisoner came to his place and he hired him for three months at 8s per week. On the Sunday, following however, prisoner left without saying that he should not come back again. While he was with witness, witness bought from him a silver watch for £1 5s and prisoner left in witness's house a light tweed coat. The watch and coat produced were the same and still bore the marks witness put on them.

Samuel Holt, Chief Constable of Newcastle, deposed that he apprehended the prisoner in the street at Newcastle early on the morning of the 25th April. When prisoner, in reply to witness's questions denied that he had ever been at Muswellbrook, but said that he had been four days in Maitland and had moved from place to place down the river till he reached Newcastle. On being asked if he had a watch, the prisoner, after some hesitation took a silver watch out of his waist coat pocket. The watch produced was the same and prisoner said he got it from Sydney nine years ago. After prisoner had been brought before the bench and was ordered to be forwarded to Muswellbrook, he admitted to the lock-up keeper that he had been at Muswellbrook in company with two other men and the man who was killed. He spoke of him as Dick Connolly but he added that he was not the man who killed him. This was in answer to a remark of the lock-up-keeper, which witness did not distinctly hear.

---

[19] Collins: To cause blood or lymph to escape into the surrounding tissue from their proper vessels.

Richard L Jenkins deposed that on his return from Sydney he delivered the watch produced to Connolly. He had taken it to Sydney to be repaired for a man named Hutton and, on his return, delivered it to Connolly by Hutton's desire. Connolly left the station about the 7th April 1848. (This was the watch identified by Ryan).

This closed the case for the prosecution.

Mr Purefoy, who had cross-examined nearly all the witness, recalled Chief Constable Fox who stated that he showed prisoner, in Muswellbrook Courthouse, the watch produced (that sold to Ryan) when the prisoner in reply to his question as to what he knew of it.

His Honour could not allow a statement of the prisoner in his own favour to be received, unless it was simply a declaration accompanying an act. A reply to a question was not of that nature.

Mr Purefoy recalled Mr Caldwell, who deposed that pen; ink and paper were asked for and obtained by Connelly and the prisoner, but for what purpose he did not know.

William Riley was recalled by his Honour, but could not identify either of the watches as the one he parted with to one of the two men.

Mr Purefoy addressed the jury for the defence. It was his duty now to offer to them some observations on the evidence that had been adduced, but he should detain them as short a time as possible, consistent with his duty to the prisoner.

It appeared to him that the question of most importance to them to determine in this case was as to the identity of the prisoner, which the evidence did not conclusively show, to his apprehension. He need not tell them that it was a well understood maxim of the laws of England, that where a doubt was felt by the jury, they should give the prisoner the benefit of the doubt. He thought he could satisfy them that by no means such conclusive and satisfactory evidence of the prisoner's identity as should lead them to the irresistible conclusion that he was the companion of the unfortunate man Connelly.

Any inconsistency in the chain of evidence put before them to prove that fact, should induce them to doubt the correctness of the conclusion sought to be established. The learned counsel then went at considerable length through the evidence, pointing out to them how difficult it was to believe that a man who had been seen prisoner for so short a time could so positively identify him as Maguire had done. In addition, that the actions of the prisoner subsequently, were quite different from what might be expected from a man who had committed so serious a crime and who would naturally be anxious to escape and keep himself concealed.

It was no doubt pretty clearly proved that the prisoner had some dealings afterwards with property that had belonged to Connelly, but there was a wide difference between believing that fact and concluding that he was his murderer, as it was clear that some transaction took place between them at Mr Caldwell's.

No appearance of blood was described as having been seen on the prisoner's dress, and so far from avoiding Mr Fox when he met him; he turned round to ask him a question.

His Honour, in summing up, repeated to the jury the substance of the two counts in the indictment, and stated that in one the prisoner was charged with having inflicted the wounds with an unknown blunt instrument, and in the other with an axe, while in both he was charged with thus having designedly and with malice aforethought killed and murdered Richard Connelly, otherwise called Richard King.

They had first to enquire whether a man called Richard Connolly, otherwise Richard King, had met with his death, and in the manner set forth in the indictment, for if he had, the law implied that a man so killed had been killed by design, and by malice aforethought, and had therefore been murdered; leaving it to the person charged with the crime to prove, if he could, that death was not caused by malice aforethought. For no doubt men might be killed and by design, yet without malice, as for instance, by a person in defence of his own life. But in the present case, the prisoner had not been able to call any evidence, and they consequently were left to imply that death was caused by malice aforethought.

His Honour then gave an abstract of the evidence as to the finding of the body, its appearance, its being identified as that of Richard Connolly, and the doctor's evidence as to the wounds, and that either of them would have caused death. He called their attention to the fact that the proof was that the wounds were on the left side and back of the head instead of the left side and front, as laid in the indictment, but he thought this was immaterial, and the indictment was sustained if it was proved that death was caused by wounds on the head.

He thought, therefore, that there was evidence for their consideration that Richard Connolly had met with his death in the manner set forth; and the question remained at whose hands he had met with his death. For it was hardly conceivable, and there was no evidence to lead to the supposition that deceased had inflicted the wounds himself. The question was then, was the prisoner the person who inflicted the wounds, and caused Connolly's death. In addition, here he would repeat the intimation of the Solicitor General that the case was one entirely of circumstantial evidence, and one, therefore, specially calling for their most careful attention. It had been said that circumstantial evidence was stronger than direct, as circumstances could not lie; but he could not assent to this position, for, although circumstances could not lie, yet the witnesses to them might, equally as much as to direct evidence. He therefore thought that direct evidence was much superior to circumstantial, and that in all cases of circumstantial evidence the jury had a more than usually solemn duty to perform, particularly where life was concerned. He would call on them, therefore, to weigh the evidence most carefully, noting the manner of each witness when giving it. In a civil case the duty of a jury was to consider on which side there was a preponderance of evidence, and to give their verdict accordingly; but in criminal cases their duty was far difficult, for unless they were satisfied of the guilt of the prisoner beyond any reasonable doubt, they must give him the benefit of the doubt, and acquit him.

They should not certainly, if any slight difficulty in the evidence presented itself, catch at it and abandoning their duty to the community, at once give a verdict for the prisoner, but should carefully compare and test it with the remainder of the evidence, and then, if they could not get over the doubt, give the prisoner the benefit of it. He would repeat to them the opinion of an eminent English judge, who told a jury that they must not only, before returning a verdict of guilty, feel that the evidence was consistent with the idea of the prisoner's guilt, but that it was inconsistent with any other conclusion, so as to lead them to the necessary and inevitable conclusion of the prisoner's guilt.

He cautioned them to dismiss from their minds anything they might have heard or read outside relating to the case before them, and to be guided only by the evidence laid before them by the Solicitor General. If that evidence left any reasonable doubt on their minds as to the prisoner's guilt, they must acquit him, for the question for them was not whether he was guilty, but whether he was proved guilty. His Honour, then gave a brief abstract of the evidence, and finished by reading over the whole as given, cautioning the jury particularly to be cautious as to the evidence of identity; and inviting them, if they felt any difficulty after having retired, to return to ask him for any information.

The jury retired at four o'clock, and returned in about half an hour with a verdict of guilty.

When asked, in the usual form, whether he had anything to urge why sentence should not be passed on him, the prisoner, whose manner throughout the trial had been quiet and somewhat depressed, said in a distinct and resolute tone that he was innocent of the crime; he urged that his name had been altered; that he had gone to the Peel River looking for a woman and was still looking for her when he returned down the country, when he left Mr Ryan's service and went to Newcastle, and that he found her in Newcastle lockup, and was waiting to see her when he was accosted by Mr Holt.

He said that he was twenty miles from Muswellbrook at the time of the murder was said to have been committed; that Riley and Maguire had not told the truth; but that all the other witnesses had. Finally, he reasserted his innocence of the crime, and said that those were the last words he should speak.

His Honour impressively addressed the prisoner, expressing his entire concurrence in verdict of the jury, and his hope that the prisoner would, if he were guilty, as all who had heard his trial must believe, make all the reparation he could to the community he had outraged by confessing his crime, in order that no other person might hereafter be accused of having committed the fearful deed. He could hold out no hopes of mercy to him in this world, and urged him to repent and seek the consolations of religion. It was now his painful duty to pass the sentence of the law upon him which was, that he should be taken to the place whence he came, and thence on a day to be appointed to the place of execution, and there to be hanged till he was dead.

The prisoner heard the sentence quite unmoved.

GEORGE WATERS WARD

Maitland Mercury 3rd March 1849

The warrant for the execution of George Waters Ward, convicted at the late Circuit Court of the murder of Richard Connelly, has been received by the authorities here. Ward is to be hung at the Maitland Gaol on Monday, the 19th March.

EXECUTION OF GEORGE WATERS WARD

Maitland Mercury 21st March 1849

On Monday morning George Waters Ward, convicted at the late Maitland Circuit Court of the murder of Richard Connelly, was executed inside the walls of Maitland gaol, in the presence of several hundred persons, including a great number of children and some women.

About five minutes past nine o'clock Ward was brought out from the gaol into the yard accompanied by the Rev. Mr Rusden (who had been with him since six o'clock that morning), C Prout Esq. the Under Sheriff, E D Day Esq., Dr Wilton, Mr Tristrem and others. The Rev. Mr Rusden read prayers, in which Ward joined with apparent fervour. Having reached the scaffold, Mr Rusden knelt down with the unfortunate man, and passed some minutes in prayer, Ward audibly joining in the responses.
About twelve minutes past nine Ward mounted the scaffold, Mr Rusden still accompanying him, and the executioner following.

On reaching the platform Ward called out in a clear firm voice, "Good bye Mr Tristrem, God bless you and you all," looking round on the crowd. Having engaged in prayer with Mr Rusden for a minute or two, Ward addressed the crowd assembled nearly as follows:

> My friends, I am going to die this day, and I hope that you will take warning by me and keep from drink, and that if any of you ever give evidence in court of justice you will speak the truth. I am not going to accuse anyone, but I will only say that some spoke the truth on my trial, and some spoke false. I die in peace with all the world, and in the hope of a better life. I pray for all you all, and I hope you will all take warning by my example.

The executioner then fastened the rope round Ward's neck, and put a white cap over his head and face, during which Mr Rusden continued praying and Ward joining with him. Mr Rusden then left the scaffold, and the bolt being drawn, the wretched man fell, and died after struggling convulsively for a few minutes. Ward's bearing on the scaffold was firm and composed throughout.

It will be observed that in his last address Ward did not say a word as to whether he was guilty or innocent. We believe he had, to all who visited him during his confinement, maintained his innocence of the murder of Connelly, and on Sunday morning he added that within a year he felt assured that his innocence would be made clear to all. In the course of Sunday, however, Mr Prout, the Under Sheriff, arrived with the death warrant, which he read to Ward; and in the course of conversation with the unfortunate man, Mr Prout urged him to tell the truth before he died.

Ward asserted his innocence, and complained that the witness McGuire had not sufficiently identified him as one of the two men he saw at the fire. Mr Prout remarked that there was so much evidence against him, altogether irrespective of McGuire's that no one could doubt his guilt, and that another proof had since been afforded, insomuch as Dr Jenkins's gold watch had been offered for sale in Maitland. Ward eagerly replied that that was impossible, for he could prove that it never had been offered for sale in Maitland. Mr Prout immediately replied that that answer had condemned him, for how could he possibly know whether the watch had been presented for sale if he did not know where it was; it was ascertained that the murdered man had taken this watch before he left, and now he had admitted that he knew where the watch was. Ward made no reply, but sat down trembling and visibly disconcerted. After that moment, we understand, he made no further professions of innocence.

THE LATE GEORGE WATERS WARD

Maitland Mercury 24th May 1849

George Waters Ward though silent as to Connelly, confessed that he had been a very great sinner; that he had over and over again, broken the commandments of his God, and that he deserved to die. He set himself, therefore, to seek reconciliation and forgiveness, and prepared to meet his God. He suffered with firmness, but with great penitence and sorrow for his past life. It had been reported by some that he was a hardened man. It is a pity that such persons, instead of hardening the hearts of others, do not endeavour to soften their own. Had they been present in his cell on Saturday, when, after prayers, he took his last leave of some of his fellow-prisoners, and heard him, in his plain strong language, and with rude eloquence, warn them against the sin of drunkenness, which had brought him to an untimely end, and would them, unless they reformed their ways, these people would have acknowledged that he had a heart to feel for others as well as for himself. He left the following statement behind, which is published at his request, and in his own words, with only a few amendments, here and there, in the spelling and grammar.

(Written by G W Ward, under Sentence of Death) Maitland Gaol, March 9 1849.

For a solemn warning to others, I am going to tell them the first steps of vice that has at last brought me to this place on confinement, where, in a few days, the Sheriff will come and demand my body, and lead me to execution.

I was born in Dublin in the year 1810; my father's name James Ward, and my mother's Anne Waters. I was brought over to Bath in England in 1813, and my good old grandmother took me, and when I was old enough put me to school and had me taught to know good from bad. When I was 13 years, she had me confirmed and bound me apprentice to a stonemason, but I had to stop with her at nights and all Sundays, when I used to go to church with her; so, my grandmother did all she could for me. She was very tender of me, too tender. But, at the age of 16 I took to drinking and unhappily for me, soon after my good old grandmother died and I soon became worse for drinking; and the next step I took was a woman. By my grandmother's death, I came into all her little property – her furniture and £24 in money. My mother wished me to come home and live with her and the family, but I would not. I was now 18 years of age and thought I would be my own master and I stuck to bad company and they lead me from bad to worse. I do not blame the rum or the women, but I blame myself most, for I always knew when I was doing right from wrong. I hope all you that know me or hear of my death, will take my advice and keep from rum; for rum drinking, had brought me into every trouble and at last to this confinement and sentence of death. I know that plenty will say, "It is my own fault," but take the heed, lest you fall, for no man that is given to drinking is safe; he is safe only in a gaol, where there is plenty of water, and someone to look after him for we are poor weak creatures when left to ourselves. For all the time I was drinking, I know that it was doing me harm and when I kept bad company that I was doing that I ought not to have done and I am leaving undone the things I ought to have done. But there is no health in me.

March 10th. I feel very low in spirits this morning, but after I had read a little and came to know and consider how my blessed Lord Jesus Christ suffered for me, I soon became better and began again to write these few lines; as I know my last hour is approaching this is all I can do. On reading over what I wrote yesterday it called to my mind what I was reading in a book the other day – "Be sure your sins will find you out." A man may escape for a few days or years, but at last God will put him to the stand and then you can think on those words, "Behold your sins have found you out." We might pass men, but we cannot escape God and if we are not found out in one crime, sooner or later another will overtake us and perhaps an end to your life as it has to mine. I hope and pray that my blessed Lord and Saviour Jesus Christ will protect me in my last moments, and keep all that do see or hear my unhappy end. That such may not be the case of any of them. I hope and pray that you will keep the Sabbath and keep from drink or else some day when you little expect it, trouble and misfortune will come upon you and you will think on those words, "Your sins have found you out." When I was in England some years ago, I was sinking a well with a young man. He and I used to get drunk two or three times a week. His mother came one day and asked him to come home, he struck his mother on the head and she fell down almost dead. I soon got transported after this and went to the York hulk at Gosport. I had not been there only two or three months before this young man came, transported for life and he told me many times that nothing hurt him so much and weighed so heavily upon his mind as his unkindness to his mother. He died at the hulk; his name was William Wise "Honour thy father and mother." This commandment of God I have broken many times, I have been very guilty, but I hope the Lord will forgive me for all my past life and protect them that is in their bloom and teach them to be obedient and honour their parents. Be kind to old people, for you may be old yourself, mind to keep your church or your chapel and keep good company, but the less of company the better for company-keeping brings many a one into prison and from thence to the place of execution. I hope such will not be your case, but look out and be on your watch before "your sins will find you out."

[Then after the confession of sundry robberies and many sins that he committed in England, he proceeds]. I was transported for seven years in 1829. When I arrived in Van Dieman's Land I got every indulgence that any prisoner could expect. I held a situation under government over the gangs employed on the roads and I always bore a good character by my officers that were placed over me. But drink got me into trouble and trouble drove me back again to drink, until I got that way that I was not fit for anything. All this time I led a very bad life and after I was married, I was worse than before. My wife, she did bad, but I did ten times worse. Still, if I had taken her advice, I should not have been here under sentence of death. I hope no one will cast any frown on my wife on account of me, for there is no blame on her part; God bless her and the dear boy, is my last prayer for them.

There is one thing I wish for to remark, that is, I never did wrong to anyone except I was in drink; and I can say from the bottom of my heart, that drink is the mother of all vice; and I hope that you will all keep from drink before your sins find you out.

But I have been a very great sinner, a great drunkard, and unkind to my wife; I have broken all the commandments of my God, all but one. "Thou shalt not covet thy neighbour's wife;" this crime I am very guilty of, and have been ever since I came to years to do mischief and commit crime. Thou shalt not commit adultery," this crime I have committed many times out of number; but I hope the Lord will have mercy on my soul and teach others not to follow my steps, for I am a great sinner. "Thou shalt not steal," this I am very guilty of, and getting drunk on Sunday.
I hope the Lord will forgive me of all my past life, and I am very thankful that I was not cut off when I was drunk and not having time to ask for mercy for my wicked life, which is now come to an end.

The Lord Jesus Christ bless the ministers of his word and I hope that all their labour is not in vain. The Lord bless and keep Rev Rusden and his family, when I am dead and gone. The Lord bless the gaoler of Newcastle and Maitland and all of the officers that have been placed over me. The Lord bless and keep and defend my fellow-prisoners. The Lord Bless us all. Amen.

Then follow sundry pious ejaculations and short sentences of Scripture, concluding with a very affecting prayer, of his own composition, in which he most earnestly entreats for mercy and forgiveness.

Reader! Would'st thou believe, if one rose from the dead? Then lay to heart these words from the grave.

Connolly was buried by the Rev. R G Boodle, Church of England minister, who recorded the following in the parish records; 'Conolly (sic), a traveller, died 14th April 1848 and buried in the C of E cemetery, Muswellbrook on the 17th April 1848, found murdered.' There is no headstone.

Did George Waters Ward cause the death of Richard Connolly and if so, was it murder?

Points to consider:

- Chief Constable Fox stated the back of Connolly's skull was beaten in, there were three holes in it. What was used to kill Connolly? it was an axe, tomahawk or very sharp-edged stone. At the Maitland Circuit Court Ward was indited as killing Connolly with an unknown blunt instrument or an axe. Dr Thomas Fowler deposed that the wound on the temple was caused by a sharp instrument and the wound on the back of the head by a blunt object. Were two people involved with the death of Connolly? There is no mention in the evidence of Fox of a search for the murder weapon.

- Fox in his evidence provides different locations for Connolly's body and state of dress.

- Body found in a gully covered over with a rug and some branches.

- Dead man lying in Muswell Brook Creek. Removed a dark rug that covered portion of the body and a cap that was on the head.

- Body lying on the face in a shallow waterhole. Covered with a dark rug, when removed, body had a red cap on the head. A shirt was rolled up round the neck and rest of body was naked.

- Why the varying locations for the body and state of dress. No mention of a red cap by any of the people who saw Ward and Connolly alive.

- Thomas Maguire is an interesting witness. Why was he reluctant to give evidence to Fox? What was his business in Muswellbrook? What was in his bundle that he lost?

- Fox stated that on returning to Muswellbrook he was hailed by a bullock driver who told him he had just discovered a man lying dead in the bush. Yet when Edward Avery, the bullock driver, gave evidence in

Maitland, he stated after he and Thomas Ward[20] discovered the body they returned to Muswellbrook and report to the magistrates, later took Fox to the spot.

- George Waters Ward was at his own admission not a law-abiding person, but he went to the gallows claiming he was innocent of the charge of murder. What do you think – guilty or not guilty?

Muswellbrook in the 1860s.

[20] Thomas Ward was a bullock driver travelling with Avery.

CASE 13 - 1849 **MUSWELLBROOK**

FLASH JEMMY **DECEASED VICTIM**

OLD BRANDY **ACCUSED OF MURDER**
JEMMY **ACCUSED OF MURDER**

MURDER NEAR MUSWELLBROOK
Maitland Mercury Wednesday 11th April 1849

We regret to have to announce the murder of a very intelligent Aboriginal named Jemmy, well-known on the Hunter as "Flash Jemmy" often employed about the neighbourhood of Muswellbrook at breaking in horses. It appeared that on Wednesday night last Jemmy, his gin, and child, who belong to the Muswellbrook tribe of blacks, were camped with some blacks of the Gammon Plains and Merton tribes, about a quarter of a mile from the township, and that about nine o'clock at night two blacks of the Merton tribe, named Old Brandy and Jemmy, came up to the camp, and without speaking a word, threw their boomerangs at Flash Jemmy, which cut his abdomen open; they then beat him with their boomerangs until he died. From the fact of the deceased being so well known as a very intelligent well-disposed aboriginal, the inhabitants here regret that the authorities cannot interfere to bring the two murderers to justice.

No report of burial in C of E parish records.

The reason for lack of action by authorities was that until 1876, a person had to take a religious oath to give evidence in an NSW court. Aboriginal people were not considered able to take a religious oath and therefore could not give evidence[27].

CASE 14 -1849 **SCONE**

WILLIAM MARRAH **DECEASED VICTIM, shepherd employed by Francis Little**

JOSEPH MARSH **ACCUSED MURDERER, hut keeper for Joseph Little, Scone, settler**

PERSONS FOR THE PROSECUTION
John Dunn **constable, Scone**
Thomas Boulton
Thomas Fowler **surgeon**
Henry Smith **innkeeper, Scone**
John Bingle **settler**

PERSONS FOR THE DEFENCE
Owen Mayne **employed by Francis Little, settler**
Brian Maloney **called, but did not appear**

MURDER OF UNKNOWN AT STATION OF JOSEPH LITTLE, SCONE
Maitland Mercury 18th July 1849

The Bench of Magistrates at Scone were occupied the whole of this day, investigating a charge of wilful murder, preferred against a man of the name of Joseph Marsh, hut keeper to Francis Little

On Tuesday (yesterday) morning Marsh, after partaking of breakfast at Mr Henry Smith's inn, Scone, went behind the bar, and told him he had murdered a man at the same station (about three miles from Scone) with a tomahawk, and that he intended murdering two more had they come in his way, giving their names.

Mr Smith at first thought the man was romancing, but as the man appeared perfectly sober, Mr Smith sent for a constable and the moment he arrived, March held out his hands to be handcuffed. He related to the constable the manner in which he perpetrated the deed with a tomahawk, the place in which he would find the instrument, and other particulars. He stated he gave the unfortunate man two blows, one across the nose, and the other across the temple.

The deceased man, on examination by Dr Fowler, showed a horrid spectacle. The first blow having divided the upper jaw from ear to ear and which might have been inflicted by such an instrument as the one produced. The second dividing the left temporal and the greater part of the frontal bones, penetrating into the substance of the brain to the depth of about two inches. Dr F. stated that either of the wounds was sufficient to cause instant death. He fully believed that when the blows were inflicted the deceased was asleep, judging from the position of the man and the bed clothes being in their proper place, and also from the garments of the deceased, even to the boots, being placed as if he had gone to bed in the usual way.

The prisoner has not made any further disclosures today, but last evening in the lock-up he attempted to destroy himself by bleeding himself to death in the bend of the elbow with two needles, which he had concealed in his hat and had not medical attendance been close at hand, he no doubt would have accomplished his purpose, as his voice brought the keepers to his cell, when he was found nearly exhausted from loss of blood.

The prisoner is remanded for further evidence to corroborate his statement. The only cause he can give for committing the deed is that the deceased "Marrah", stole some of his sennit[21] (he being a hat maker) and clothes. There was no blood on the prisoner's clothes although the blows must have been struck with great force. The tomahawk is smeared with the brains of the deceased and there is blood on the handle. The bench has issued a warrant for another man called the "Native", but the prisoner states he had no hand in the murder, but was in the vicinity of the hut and was warned not to approach it by the prisoner on the night of the murder. Every circumstance mentioned by the prisoner has been found on examination strictly in accordance with the facts as far as ascertained.

Maitland Circuit Court, Murder, Before his Honour Mr Justice Manning

---

[21] http://en.wikipedia.org/wiki/Sennit **Sennit** (also **sinnet**) is a type of cordage made by plaiting strands of dried fibre or grass. It can be used ornamentally in crafts, like a kind of *macramé*, or to make straw hats.

Maitland Mercury 11th September 1849

Joseph Marsh was indicted for assaulting William Marrah at Middlebrook [near Scone] on the 9th July 1849, and with a tomahawk, striking him on the left side of the head and face, inflicting divers mortal wounds, whereof he instantly died and for thus wilfully murdering the said William Marrah.
The prisoner made an application to the Court stating that he was unprepared to go to trial and wanted two witnesses whom he had applied for to the gaoler. On inquiry, it appeared that the prisoner had not asked for these witnesses till a few days ago and that although one of them was at the time a prisoner of the gaol, who had been since discharged, he never named this to the gaoler. His Honour, having inquired into the circumstances, said it appeared to him that the application was not made because these witnesses were necessary, but merely in order to postpone the case and he must therefore allow the case to go on.

The Attorney General stated the particulars of the case to the jury.

It appeared from the evidence of Henry Smith, John Dunn, Thomas Boulton, John Bingle and Dr Thomas Fowler that the prisoner was a watchman in the employment of Mr Little and that Marrah was a shepherd with the same employer. On the night of the 9th July 1849 the prisoner and a man named Brian Maloney went to Mr Smith's inn and got a bed. In the morning, they had breakfast and after breakfast a glass of liquor each in the bar. They had been in the bar a few minutes when prisoner who was perfectly sober went inside the counter and told Mr Smith that he had murdered a man at the station the previous night and if he had not killed the man the man would have killed him. He stated he struck him two blows with a tomahawk, one across the nose and the other on the head that settled him and that if that had not settled him, he would have given him five blows. He gave himself into Mr Smith's charge and would not stir from the place till he was taken into custody.

Mr Smith sent for the police and Constable Dunn and another constable came, to whom the prisoner made a similar statement and described the position in which they would find Marrah lying and where they would find the tomahawk. Dunn took him to the lock-up and on the way the prisoner told him that Marrah had robbed his gunyah[22] a few days before of a blanket and that he had also come to his gunyah and set fire to the rug in front of it and burnt it and the things he was lying on and that Marrah kept the station in an uproar.

Dunn then went to the station and found Marrah lying on his back on a bed on the floor, exactly as prisoner had described. The body was covered over with a blanket and lifting it, Dunn saw two severe wounds on the head, one across the front of the face and the other on the temple. A great quantity of blood had run from the wounds on the bed and floor.

Boulton had seen Marrah in good health about the 5th July; he did not know his Christian name. He was with the body at the churchyard when Dr Fowler came and looked at the body. Mr Bingle deposed that when the prisoner was committed for trial, he made the voluntary statement produced after being cautioned. This statement was read and in it the prisoner confessed that he murdered William Marrah and that no one assisted him or had any hand in it.

Dr Fowler examined the body in the hut and found two deep wounds, one on the left temporal bone and one dividing the cheek-bone from the upper jaw. They were so deep that either would have been sufficient to cause death. From the position of the body and the general appearances, he was of the opinion that the blows were struck when Marrah was lying on his bed, the tomahawk produced would inflict such wounds. The prisoner afterwards attempted to destroy himself in the lockup and he told Dr Fowler, who attended him that Marrah had several times robbed him. The witnesses who visited the hut said there was no appearance there of any struggle. A bottle, half full of rum, was found by Dunn outside the hut and inside was found a case bottle which contained gin. In the course of Mr Smith's evidence, he stated that after the prisoner had told him of murdering Marrah, the prisoner, while waiting for the police, told him also that Maloney had robbed him while they were sleeping together in his house the previous night and that if he could have found an opportunity he would have cut Maloney's throat while they were at breakfast together. Maloney was present when this was said and appeared quite stunned at Marsh's revelations.

The prisoner called Owen Mayne who deposed that he had been in Mr Little's service, but left the station the morning before the murder. There had been some liquor occasionally brought to the hut, there had been some quarrelling between Marrah and John Maloney on the Sunday night before witness left when Marrah refused to fight Maloney. Marrah had stolen some of witness's things previously, but witness and Marrah never quarrelled.

---

[22] Macquarie: Small rough hut or shelter.

On that Sunday night there was liquor drank in the hut, Marrah bringing the second lot, there was no quarrelling after that was brought.

The prisoner then called John Maloney but he did not appear. Mr Smith stated that was not the same man as Brian Maloney.

The prisoner said he was unable to address the jury, but he was innocent of the charge. A statement which had been written by him in gaol was read by the Clerk of Arraigns in which the prisoner detailed a series of drinking bouts which he alleged took place in Marrah's hut and in which Marrah threatened Mayne, Maloney and himself. That on the night of the 9th there were only Marrah, a young man called "The Native" and himself. Marrah, during supper abused and threatened him and after supper produced some liquor of which all partook, but Marrah became so violent and outrageous in his threats that at length "The Native" left. Marrah became more violent still, but at length stripped and lay down on his bed, still threatening and at last he (prisoner) provoked by these constant attacks and seeing Marrah reaching out his hand for the tomahawk, seized it and struck him two blows, being convinced that Marrah would take his life if he did not prevent him.

After this statement was read, the prisoner briefly addressed the jury, saying that this was the strict truth and that he was convinced Marrah would have killed him if he had not struck the blows when he did.

His Honour summed up, stating that the principal question for the jury to decide was whether or not the crime was committed under circumstances that made it a case of manslaughter instead of murder, as no doubt could be felt that Marrah died from wounds inflicted by the prisoner. His Honour read authorities to guide the jury in forming their conclusion. In this case, the evidence almost entirely rested on the prisoner's own statements and therefore the jury would take into consideration the whole of the statements made by him. Those for as well as against him, attaching what credit they thought due to them and to each part, and enquiring also how much of these statements was borne out by the evidence brought forward. In this respect the evidence as to the position in which Marrah was found lying was important. His Honour having laid down the principles to guide the jury, read the evidence over at length.

The jury retired for ten minutes and returned with a verdict of guilty. The prisoner was remanded for sentence.

SAME DAY - SENTENCED

The sentence of the court was then prayed on Joseph Marsh, convicted of the murder of William Marrah.

His Honour impressively sentenced the prisoner, addressing him nearly as follows: Joseph Marsh, you have been found guilty of the dreadful crime of wilful murder and it is now my painful duty to pass on you the last sentence of the law. If I could see the slightest reason to doubt whether I ought to pass sentence of death I would delay it and reflect most seriously on your case, but my duty appears clear. I have absolutely no alternative. Painful as it is to be in any way an instrument, though most innocently, and in the course of a simple duty, in sacrificing the life of a fellow creature. A man such as myself with the same mortal body, the same immortal soul, with the like hopes and fears, sensibility to pain and value for life – my bounden duty is to award the sentence of death and I cannot shrink from it. It is the law, not your judge that fixes your doom.

I cannot dilate on the enormity of your offence – to which intoxicating liquors have probably led you – or harass you with lengthened observations on the evidence. It is useless now. Nor will I address you on that most important topic; your spiritual welfare in another world. The subject of religion, of God's mercy to the penitent through the mediation of the Saviour will come with infinitely more force from the reverend gentleman who will attend you and will be brought more home to your heart in the solitude of your cell than in the presence of a multitude in open court. But one thing I would observe and would have you reflect on with gratitude, that you exit from this world will be under more happy auspices that that of the unfortunate victim of your ill-regulated passion.

He was sent – probably whilst in his sleep – with all his sins thick upon him, with no opportunity even for one penitent thought, for one short prayer of mercy. You, if the sentence, which I am about to award, be carried into execution, will have time to repent and seek forgiveness at the throne of mercy – a better termination probably, to this transitory life that if you had died in your bed without the awful warning and time for preparation which will now immediately precede your death. It is even yet possible that your life may be spared. The law has provided a fountain of mercy in the person of the Governor, as the Queen's representative and before him and his council your case will be laid and fully and mercifully considered. But I must warn you not to indulge hopes, for I confess that I see no grounds for such hope at present and I earnestly advise you to surrender your heart and mind to the teaching of your spiritual instructor and to make the utmost use of the short time that you may count upon as yours in this world.

It is now my duty to pass on you the last sentence of the law, which is that you be taken hence to the gaol from whence you came, and from thence to such place of execution and at such time as the Governor shall appoint and be there hanged by the neck till your body be dead. May God have mercy on your immortal soul? The prisoner was then removed from the dock.

SMH 17 October 1849: Joseph Marsh who was tried and convicted of murder at the last Maitland assizes, before His Honor, Mr Justice Manning, and was sentenced to death, has had his sentence commuted to ten years labour on the roads, or other public works of the colony, the first two years in irons.

In 1853, Joseph Marsh was listed as an Overseer at Cockatoo Island[28].

The deceased William Marrah, aged 40 years was buried in St Luke's C of E cemetery, Scone[29].

Justice Manning.

CONCLUSION

During the period between 1837 and 1849 information concerning fourteen murders was found in various records, mainly newspapers. The deaths took place from Ravensworth to Scone and west to Turee. There may have been further cases, but the details have not been located.

In two of the cases examined, the officials believed that persons were murdered, but the murderers were never identified and brought to trial. In one, the identity of the murdered person was not established.

The identity of the murderer of Constable Fox was established, but he was never captured and it is unknown how he met his end. In two cases the deceased were Aboriginals and killed by fellow Aboriginals and it appears that is where the officials left the cases. Four men were charged with murder, but the jury found them not guilty of murder, instead found it was manslaughter.

Five men were found guilty of murder and were hung. There were six men charged with aiding and abetting murder, five were hung, one had his sentence commuted.

Well, dear reader, what do you think? Where all the men that were hung guilty as charged or is there some doubt in your mind.

My thoughts:

Case 1: James McKeel charged with murder of Michael McShane, jury found him guilty of manslaughter, correct decision.
Case 2: Person or persons unknown murdered John Bydell. To me it is not clear if he was murdered. Did he ride into a limb of a tree. Case not investigated thoroughly.
Case 3: Edward Tufts charged with murder of John Jones. I found this case disturbing. Did Tufts kill Jones or was it someone else? If it was Tufts, did he kill with 'with malice prepense or aforethought'? It appears that rum played a part in the running of the station and that Jones was a violent man. Was it self defence on Tufts part. I believe Tufts was not guilty of murder.
Case 4: John Hobson accused of the murder of Constable Fox, but never captured and it is unknown what happened to him.
Case 5: If you thought James Walker was guilty then I believe you were correct. The evidence presented shows him to be a very nasty person who cared little for anyone else. Mason and Walker were found guilty of aiding and abetting Martin in the crime. Did they go willingly or coerced? They certainly would not have expected someone to be murdered. Walker escaped the gallows because of his treatment of the women and children. Mason was not so lucky, really, he was only a boy and I feel, under the influence or in fear of Walker.
Case 6: If you agreed with the jury of 1840, I believe you were correct.
Case 7: Again, the accused made a deliberate act to kill Constable Rutledge and was guilty of murder.
Case 8: Here there was a deceased person who was most likely killed with a knife and a deliberate attempt to dispose of the body. We have limited information, but it appears the authorities did not make an effort to find the murderer or identify the body.
Case 9: The white man had strong reasons for disposing of Tommy and this should have been strongly investigated.
Case 10: The case of Joseph Palfrey raises suspicions that there was another person or persons involved in his death. John Purcell suffered gross provocation, but James Brady had much to gain from the death of Palfrey and removal of Purcell.
Case 11: I believe the jury made the correct decision, what did you think?
Case 12: The evidence in this case is contradictory and Ward never made an admission of guilt. I wonder why Maguire was so evasive. I have a feeling the wrong person was hung.
Case 13: This is a difficult case to make a decision. Was Tommy punished by the Aboriginals for breaking an Aboriginal law? This is still happening today in areas where Aboriginal law is practiced. An offender will be punished twice, European law and Aboriginal law.
Case 14: I believe the jury made the correct decision and Marsh was guilty of murder; his sentence should not have been reduced to manslaughter.

Here you have 14 cases where someone has been killed. There were no case where the deceased or accused were female, just an observation. You have been exposed to life in the bush in the 1840 that was far removed from that of the larger population areas. Some of the stations had more people living on them than Muswellbrook or Scone.

Not only have you been provided with information regarding the legal system then, but exposed to how people lived. I hope you have been enlightened.

BIBLIOGRAPHY

Andrews, E, 2007, Murder at *Terragong*, published by the author.
Andrews, E, 2012, *The Blaxland Family, In the Upper Hunter*, published by author.
Butlin, NG; Cromwell, CW; Suthern, KL eds. 1987, *General Return Convicts in NSW 1837*, ABGR, Sydney.
Cameron, R & Job, K, 1993, *Around the Black Stump*, Council of the Shire of Coolah, Coolah.
Castles, A, 1982, *An Australian Legal History*, Law Book Co., Sydney.
Haynes, F, 1984, *Cassilis, The Frontier Village*, publisher not named.
Malor, J, 1969, *Outline of Law in Australia*, Law Book Co., Sydney.
Milliss, R, 1994, *Waterloo Creek*, University of NSW Press, Sydney.
Neal, D, 1991, *The Rule of Law in a Penal Colony*, Cambridge University press, Cambridge.
Tickle, R, nd, *St Heliers Convict Register*, MSLFHS, Muswellbrook.
Tickle, R, 2015, *Kayuga Cemetery*, MSLFHS, Muswellbrook.
Wilkinson, W H, 1860, *Plunkett's Australian Magistrate*, JJ Moore, Sydney.
Wood, W A, 1972, *Dawn in the Valley*, Wentworth Books, Surry Hills.
Woods, G D, 2002, *A History of Criminal Law in New South Wales, The Colonial Period,1788-1900*, Federation Press, Annandale.

ENDNOTES

---

[1] Hunter Estates, Vol. 1 2013, NSW Office of Environment & Heritage.
[2] RAHS *History Magazine*, March 2025 No. 163.John Hurbert Plunkett: Australia's Unsung Hero, Mark Tedeschi, p.12. https://adb.anu.edu.au/biography/plunkett-john-hubert-2556.
[3] J H Plunkett, 1835, *The Australian Magistrate*, Ann Howe, Gazette, Sydney, pp.231-239.
[4] NSW Parliamentary Library Research Service: *Trial by Jury, Historical Developments.*
[5] State Archives NSW, Convict Indent Fiche 676, p.151.
[6] State Archives NSW, Col Sec, 4/2419.1, Letter 38/3004.
[7] NSW GG 4 April 1838.
[8] R Cameron & K Job, 1993, *Around the Black Stump*, Council of the Shire of Coolah, Coolah. pp. 9-18.
[9] *Sydney Gazette* 1 March 1838).
[10] NSW State Archives, Convict Indents, Fiche 673.
[11] NSW GG 14 November 1838.
[12] State Archives NSW. Muswellbrook Court of Petty Sessions, Letter Books, 1831-1851. Reel 2742.
[13] *NSW GG* 12 June 1839.
[14] *The Australian* 25 February 1841.
[15] *The Sydney Herald* 16 January 1841.
[16] State Archives NSW, Col Sec. File 4/2544.5, Letters 41/497 & 41/654.
[17] *Maitland Mercury* 28 November 1846.
[18] State Archives NSW, Convict Indents, Fiche 704, p.81. General Return of Convicts 1837. Col Sec correspondence Letter 40/257.
[19] F Haynes, 1984, *Cassilis, The Frontier Village*, publisher not named, p.60.
[20] NSW BDM Marriage 1845/67/30B. Baptism 1846/1976/32A.
[21] *SMH* 10 January 1849 & Maitland Mercury 8 August 1849.
[22] HLRV Old System Bk 14 No.362.
[23] HLRV Old System Bk 85 No.176.
[24] HLRV Old System Bk 85 No.177.
[25] *Maitland Mercury* 26 June 1847.
[26] *Maitland Mercury* 16 February 1848.
[27] 1876 40 VIC No.9, An Act for the further amendment of the Law of Evidence.
[28] *People's Advocate & NSW Vindicator* 29 October 1853.
[29] NSW BDM Burial 1849/1383/34B Scone.

INDEX

INDEX

www.ingramcontent.com/pod-product-compliance
Lightning Source LLC
LaVergne TN
LVHW070408110826
845147LV00016B/971

* 9 7 8 1 9 2 3 5 2 7 2 7 0 *